AN INTRODUCTION TO SURREALISM

AN INTRODUCTION TO SURREALISM

---

by J. H. Matthews

THE PENNSYLVANIA STATE UNIVERSITY PRESS

UNIVERSITY PARK, PENNSYLVANIA

Library of Congress Catalog Card Number 64–8083
Copyright © 1965 by The Pennsylvania State University
All rights reserved
Printed in the United States of America
by Kingsport Press, Inc.
Designed by Maxine Schein

FOR JEANNE

PREFACE

This is not a literary history; nor is it a work of criticism. This book aims rather at explication, and does not purport to estimate the achievement of Surrealism or seek to lay bare weaknesses in Surrealist thought. It has grown from a curiosity to understand that thought, however, in its implications for poetry and painting. This is not to say that the present study has as its purpose to determine the literary or artistic quality of the works Surrealism has inspired. Evaluation of these works must necessarily be preceded by a close examination of the function Surrealism reserves for them.

No one, least of all someone who has not viewed it from within, can hope fully to comprehend Surrealism. But one may reasonably aim at some clarification of the principles upon which it rests and has wished to build, some apprehension of the programme it has laid out, and some insight into the methods it has used to advance its ends. These therefore are the main preoccupations in the pages that follow.

To those for whom Surrealism is a thing of the past, an approach such as I have adopted may seem excessively cautious. However, to those who recognize that Surrealism has not yet said its last word,[1] the very inconclusiveness to which my approach leads must appear inevitable, in a discussion of a movement that can still today lay claim to considerable vitality. And this is especially true of Surrealism, which needs to be understood before it can be judged, but has been so frequently judged without being understood. So I have tried to go back to first principles, returning to the Surrealist writings and demanding of them—rather than of their commentators—the guidance needed to see where Surrealism has come from, and where it wishes to go. I have consequently allowed the Surrealists themselves an extended hearing, entrusting them with the burden of explaining the problems they have faced, and the solutions that have seemed to them most satisfactory. I have been less concerned to present the major personalities than to establish what preoccupations constitute the constants of Surrealist thought.

Accepting as my point of departure the view that Surrealism, in whatever form it has found to express itself, is merely the reflection of an attitude of mind, I have sought primarily to assemble evidence that casts light upon this attitude. Thus, when seen from this angle, the comments Surrealist writers have made upon the work of Surrealist painters assume a relevance the remarks of the art critics do not always have. For it is significant that the prefaces written by Surrealists for various exhibitions tell us more about the artists as Surrealists than as painters.[2] Drawn, therefore, from widely differing sources sometimes—and quite often from the writings of Surrealists whose contribution has been noticeably more theoretical than practical —this evidence merits presentation even when the statements from which it comes have been made in points of time many years apart. Circumstances have imposed upon the Surrealists the need to stress one aspect of their programme at some moment rather than another, but Surrealist thought has been characterized, over a period of forty years, by a remarkable continuity that it has been my purpose to emphasize.

The larger part of this book is devoted to discussing certain well-established techniques that repeated use has rendered characteristic of Surrealism in poetry and painting. This is why it has proved necessary to begin with a consideration of the issues which give these techniques their relevance and impose upon their use clearly defined limits. While it would be erroneous to suggest that technique provides the only key to the "enchanters' domain" to which the Surrealist aspires, an examination of Surrealism's ambitions and methods may very profitably be approached through an examination of the technical devices these have endowed with significance. For by considering Surrealism's techniques against the background of the general and far-reaching programme the Surrealists have promoted, one may hope to see more clearly that Surrealism is a matter of intention and not of technique; that the latter takes its meaning from the former and would be valueless without it.

The essential concern that recommends itself is the clear distinction of Surrealist thought in its continuity and vitality, and as it has found expression through certain literary and pictorial techniques. Any attempt to pre-judge developments Surrealism is free to take in the future must consequently prove immaterial. So must consideration of the degree to which Surrealism is permanently committed to any of the technical paths so far explored. Instead, I have deemed it advisable to let the Surrealists continue to speak for themselves, with no more distortion than must necessarily result from withdrawing quotations from their context.

In no literary or artistic movement has the sense of common purpose been more striking than in Surrealism. Surrealist painting and poetry complement one another, by virtue of their common fundamental intention. Surrealist painters and poets have found inspiration in collaboration, and the most recent Surrealist reviews, despite rising costs, are significantly as profusely illustrated as their pre-war counterparts. Guy Cabanel's *Maliduse* (1961) is illustrated by drawings by Mimi Parent, Adrien Dax, and Robert Lagarde—just as Eluard's *Facile* (1935) had photographs by

Man Ray and Leonora Carrington's *La Dame Ovale* (1939) collages by Ernst. In such cases pictorial material is not mere adornment. It always records the response of the artist to the feelings communicated in the text, so that word and picture become mutually illuminating. And Breton's "prose parallels" to Miró's *Constellations* show that it is not always the painter who turns to the writer for inspiration. So when Gérard Legrand speaks of certain types of Surrealist painting, and uses terms like "pure provocation," "the expansion of fabulous eroticism" and "metaphysical," [3] one may without difficulty find equivalents in the field of poetry for the work of the painters he mentions. Duchamp and Picabia— whom Legrand cites under his first heading—remind us of Péret and the early Aragon. His second group, that includes Picabia and Ernst, calls to mind Joyce Mansour, the Desnos of *La Papesse du Diable*, the Péret of *Les Couilles enragées*. The metaphysical painting of Chirico, Ernst and Masson (in *Mythologie de la Nature*, for instance), is paralleled by much that has been written by the Surrealist poets, among them, notably, Breton. So Georges Goldfayn voiced a Surrealist truth when he asserted that the problems of painting are no different from those of poetry.[4] And his words offer authority for examining at one and the same time the techniques of Surrealist art as they are evidenced in painting and poetry. For, in considering these techniques and the problems they pose, we shall find further proof that the methods favored in Surrealism have remained what the Surrealist believes they should be: not ends but means.

Grants made by the Research Board of the University of Leicester have enabled me to consult Surrealist material in the Bibliothèque littéraire Jacques Doucet, Paris, where the Librarian, M. François Chapon gave me every assistance. A grant from the Williams College 1900 Fund made possible the purchase of microfilm material from the Mary Reynolds Collection, courteously supplied by Miss Ruth E. Shoneman, Librarian of the Ryerson Library in the Art Institute of

Chicago. Additional microfilm was purchased with funds made available by the Department of French, University of Leicester. A Fulbright travel award met the expenses of a voyage to the United States and ensured me the fullest support of the Committee on International Exchange of Persons, of the Conference Board of Associated Research Councils. I am particularly indebted to Miss Mary Hoch, the Committee's Program Officer, who was especially helpful in arranging access to the Walter P. Chrysler Jr. Collection of documents from the Eluard and Dausse Surrealist Collection, deposited in the Library of the Museum of Modern Art, New York, where my work was greatly facilitated by the efficiency of the staff. During my visit to Williams College, Massachusetts, in 1960–61, the College Librarian, Mr. Willis R. Wright displayed the greatest patience in locating and obtaining books. He was most ably assisted in this task by Mrs. Dorothy Sprague and Mrs. Elizabeth Scherr. My warmest thanks are due to these three, and also to Doctor Sweetman, formerly Art Librarian in the Leicester Colleges of Art and Technology. Finally my thanks go to my wife for her unfailing encouragement and her persistent demands for clarification.

CONTENTS

DADA 1

For the sake of Progress we must destroy Art
Theo Van Doesburg

Few subjects have inspired such nonsensical comment as Surrealism. Few, that is, except Dada, which has inspired possibly more. Dadaists enjoyed over the Surrealists the advantage of being even less concerned to meet their public half-way, and even more content to meet ridicule with ridicule, to match nonsense with nonsense. Thus, stimulating though their attitude no doubt was to the Dadaists themselves, it offers little help in the attempt—be it enthusiastic, half-hearted or grudging—to establish the true significance of Dada. Indeed, the very thought of approaching Dada in a spirit of seriousness must at first glance seem paradoxical. We find ourselves wondering if the final temptation—a supreme Dada joke—Dadaism has left behind it is not that, almost fifty years after Dada became a reality, we should still be trying to define its scope and assess its meaning.[1] It would seem, in fact, that caution recommends we regard Dada as a phenomenon and accept it as such, without proposing to justify or submit it to critical examination. Yet historical necessity denies us the comfortable convenience of such conclusions. Dada made its presence felt, it is true. But it came *after* something else, and, what is more important, was replaced in its turn. Therefore, while it is beyond the scope of this study to examine in detail how Dada came to be born and how it came to die, some consideration must be given to its activity, so as to prepare for an examination of the movement which succeeded it in France: Surrealism.

For this reason, though we may without hesitation disregard much of the nonsense Dada has provoked from outsiders, we cannot afford to reject, without deliberation, the nonsense for which the Dadaists themselves were responsible. This does not necessarily mean we refuse to regard it as nonsense, and gravely accept it at its face value. But we can admit it as relevant to our purpose. In this way, its very impertinence becomes pertinent; as we see from an elementary example.

Once, when asked to relate how Dada was founded, Hans Arp replied: "I hereby declare that Tristan Tzara found the word Dada on February 8, 1916, at six o'clock in the afternoon: I was present with my twelve children when Tzara for the first time uttered this word which filled us with justified enthusiasm. This occurred in the Café de la Terrasse in Zurich and I was wearing a brioche in my left nostril." Here deliberate use of transparent untruths supporting mockery of pedantic exactitude culminates in a final fanciful detail to give Arp's statement a quality the Surrealists were soon to define as *provocation*. We see Arp defying us to believe him, and to disbelieve him. Behind his remarks with their patent facetiousness we may detect a fundamental seriousness, especially noticeable in his refusal to satisfy mere academic curiosity. Rendering explicit what his words have implied, Arp now goes on to dismiss the date of Dada's birth as essentially unimportant, when emphasizing: "What interests us is the Dada spirit and we were all Dada before Dada came into existence." [2]

Dada nonsense is, in reality, more than a smoke screen used to disguise Dada's real activities from a public deemed incapable of appreciating them. In Dada, nonsense both exteriorizes an attitude and serves the aims this attitude invests with importance. Its repeated use permits us to appreciate how true it is that Dada was not primarily a literary movement, or an artistic one. It can therefore lead us to concern ourselves with essentials; those essentials Tzara defined in a "Lecture on Dada," dating from 1921 : "It is not the technique that interests us, but the spirit." Tzara's remarks, we may note in passing, are no more than a reaffirmation of a statement made the previous year by Richard Huelsenbeck, to the effect that Dada is a state of mind.

Now the undertone of seriousness in Arp's account of the origins of Dada affects us more forcefully. Evidently, as Arp hinted, much that is irrelevant must cease to hold our attention when we realize we can begin to study Dada most successfully, not by a chronological approach that proposes to fix the date on which the word "Dada" was first used, but by regarding this word, as the Dadaists themselves did, as simply a sort of code-word. Tzara's famous 1918 *Dada Manifesto* invites us to do this, by inference at least, when it cites numerous conflicting meanings of "Dada," borrowed from several languages. Tzara, like those for whom he was spokesman, desired to reserve for Dada more freedom than would have been permissible if its title had admitted strict limitations of meaning. His manifesto therefore expressly declared that "sensibility is not constructed on the basis of a word," and all the work of the Dadaists attests the validity of his assertion.

Matters of historical precedence do not count here, as Tzara agreed when he acknowledged in *New York Dada* (1921) : "Dada existed before us." But it is worth noting that Herbert S. Gershman has convincingly demonstrated that the Dada programme owes much to the example of Italian Futurism.[3] For no Dadaist would ever have claimed Dada to be an entirely new discovery, or suggested that its characteristic expression was confined to the activity of a small group of men working at a given historical moment, in close or loose association. On the contrary, Huelsenbeck, for instance, asserted in 1920, in *En Avant Dada: Eine*

Geschichte des Dadaismus: "Everyone can be a Dadaist.
Dada is not limited to any art." His declaration continues
with a characteristic Dadaist joke, in deliberate bad taste:
"The bartender in the Manhattan Bar, who pours out Cura-
çao with one hand and gathers up his gonorrhœa with the
other, is a Dadaist. The gentleman in the raincoat, who is
about to start his seventh trip around the world, is a
Dadaist." Then an equally characteristic change of tone
returns us to seriousness: "The Dadaist should be a man
who has fully understood that one is entitled to have ideas
only if one can transform them into life—the completely
active type, who lives only through action, because it holds
the possibility of his achieving knowledge." Thus a Dadaist
may be, as Huelsenbeck assures us, "the man who rents a
whole floor at the Hotel Bristol without knowing where the
money is coming from to tip the chambermaid," [4] but he also
possesses a special sense of responsibility, reflecting a new
awareness that has led him to give a name to the state of
mind in which he finds himself, and which dictates the most
significant of his actions.

In other words, to appreciate the action the Dadaists were
impelled to take, we must begin by examining the state of
mind expressed in Dada. In order to do this, we may begin
by turning to the writings of the generally-accepted leader
of Dadaism, Tristan Tzara, in which we note how often he
has mentioned that feeling of profound disgust from which
Dada gathered strength. We may reasonably term this disgust the immediate exciting cause of Dada, for we do not
find it expressed solely in Tzara. Gabrielle Buffet-Picabia,
for instance, has commented sharply upon the self-satisfied
rationalism of the nineteenth century, followed, she says, by
"an ebullience of invention, of exploration beyond the realm
of the visible and the rational in every domain of the mind."
As a consequence, the early years of the twentieth century
appeared to her to be marked by the gradual "breaking-
down" of human, social and intellectual values that, until
then, had gone unquestioned. Here, we may be sure, lies the
explanation for that "violent disgust at the old, narrow

security," this writer detected in herself and in others of her generation: "We were all convinced of the decline of reason and its experience, and alert to the call of another reason, ✓ another logic which demanded a different experience and different symbols." [5] First Futurism then Dada, so clearly precipitated by the disgust aroused in intelligent people by the 1914–18 war, which conclusively demonstrated the invalidity of the nineteenth century's belief in progress.

Rather than join the folly of war, Huelsenbeck fled Germany, and took refuge in Switzerland. Here he met a fellow-countryman Hugo Ball, an Alsation, Arp, and two Rumanians, Tzara and Marcel Janco. All appeared to have left home for the same reason as he. None of them, Huelsenbeck has confided in *En Avant Dada,* "had much appreciation for the kind of courage it takes to get shot for an idea of a nation which is at best a cartel of pelt merchants and profiteers in ✓ leather, at worst a cultural association of psychopaths who, like the Germans, marched off with a volume of Gœthe in their knapsacks, to skewer Frenchmen and Russians on their bayonets."

If we dismiss Huelsenbeck's remarks as a rationalization of the instinct of self-preservation, we come close to doing real injustice to one of the fundamental impulses of Dada—an impulse that marked, incidentally, a notable divergence from Futurism: the categorical denial of the claims ✓ of nationalism. But if we accept his reasons as genuine, we find ourselves better placed to appreciate how Dada came to identify culture with nationalism, and to reject the one with the other. Both, in fact, became the object of contempt for the Dadaists. Both were regarded as exemplifying traditionally accepted values. And it goes without saying that these were the values that, so far as the Dadaists were concerned, events in Europe were showing to be quite meaningless. Thus Dada's attack upon culture finds its significance not so much in a form of exhibitionism, designed simply to attract attention, but rather in the refusal to admit the claims of a social organization and a mode of thought which, in the estimation of the Dadaists, had gone for too long unchallenged. Tzara's 1918 manifesto announced unequivocally: "It is only contrast that connects us to the past." No progress seemed possible until a break had been effected with all that society had accustomed the individual to accept without question. This view of things gave Dada's message a timely, exciting quality, so that the impact of Dada upon minds already inclined to question society and its usages is easy to conceive: "We spit upon humanity," cried Tzara. "We demanded the *tabula rasa,*" explains Janco.

From the very beginning, Dada's essential quality found expression in a systematic opposition, a refusal to compromise, a denial of restraint. It is significant, therefore, that in Germany Dada took on political color. For Dada questioned the very basis of society, setting out to awaken in its public a critical attitude calculated to produce beneficial results. Thus the wider implications of Dada give particular point to its activities in media where it found most dramatic expression: in literature and in art. Indeed, it is only in the broad context of Dada thought that we can fully appreciate why the Dadaists made poetry and painting the focal point of their attack upon convention. Literature and art appeared to them as the very image of society, consecrated by habit and smug self-satisfaction. How better to awaken men to a new awareness than by subjecting to ridicule the techniques and attitudes reflected in their art forms?

Dada has too often been presented as a form of unalleviated nihilism, having no impulse but to destroy, no aim but to discredit. It is frequently cited as a form of artistic suicide, leading nowhere and happy to do so. Beyond Dada, we are assured, there can be nothing. Such views are reiterated time after time, despite Tzara's affirmation—made, it is true, a number of years after Dada's demise—that Dada did not so much try to destroy art and literature as the idea people had about them.[6] Tzara's words are a clear directive to students of Dada to look beyond immediate preoccupations to fundamental aims and ultimate intentions. These are especially valuable in indicating the most profitable approach in an examination of Dada's attitude towards poetic language.

The determined opposition to language as it is habitually used for artistic communication is, beyond doubt, an expression in Dada of a break with the past and all it stands for. But it has led to the conclusion, proposed by several critics, that the Dadaists sought to undermine the very basis upon which language rests, through the denial of logic. The fourth number of the review *Dada* does indeed proclaim, "Logic no longer guides us," and Marcel Janco has emphasized that the Dadaists are concerned with the moment when "the abscesses of festering reason dissolve without trace." However it would be erroneous to equate this attitude with nihilism. For Dada turned away from reason and logic in the belief that liberation from the limitations of everyday life could not be achieved by these means. Here lies the explanation for Tzara's frequently quoted assertion, in his fifth Dada Manifesto, to the effect that the greatest mistakes which have ever been made are the poems that have been written.

Tzara, evidently, was one of those who proposed to remedy matters. He was led, in fact, to formulate the proposition that "thought is made in the mouth." In his view, true creation lies not in turning to the mind, which submits creativity to the control of logical arrangement and sequence, but in allowing thoughts to create themselves by a process making no demands upon intelligence or reflection. Considered against the background of this theory, his much publicized proposals for poetic composition may be seen to embody a residuum of seriousness. For it was Tzara who suggested the poet take a newspaper, snip its sentences up into individual words, and place these in a bag which must be shaken before the words are withdrawn once more. The result, Tzara assures us, will "resemble" the poet responsible for it.

Once again we must disengage serious intent from fantasy and wilful nonsense. Although Tzara has indeed published poems composed according to his own recipe, there seems little to be gained by a generalization of the methods suggested. Yet reflection confirms these methods to be not entirely devoid of meaning, when it is recognized that Tzara set himself the task of organizing an attack upon the very principles usually considered to supply the elements of poetic inspiration. At one sweep, inspiration, formal perfection, technical competence, and logical arrangement are all sacrificed in favor of a purely mechanical process that leaves everything to chance. This means that Tzara's suggestions have a double significance. First the poem must lose its value as the expression of the individual sensibility of its author. Second, poetic composition ceases to be the privilege and prerogative of a select few endowed with special gifts. It becomes, instead, something anyone can produce who can handle a pair of scissors. Just as the poet loses his elevated status and artistic individuality, so he loses too his sense of responsibility. By a method that reduces his participation to a minimum, he becomes not so much the creator of the poem as the medium through which the poem finds expression, thanks to the intervention of chance. Here we witness something later to become increasingly important with the emergence and clarification of Surrealist aims and techniques. But already it is possible to note something else. Tzara's instructions constitute a specific act of defiance and revolt, as significantly meaningless as his act of reading from the evening newspaper to an audience assembled to hear some of his poems. Tzara's first concern was to challenge the dignified status of poetry, to dispel the aura surrounding the very word "poem." To do so, he demonstrated that anything could be raised to the level of poetry, and the public induced to accept it as such, by the simple fact that what they are invited to hear is offered as a poem. Just as it was Dada's purpose to question the very concept of poetry and the means by which poetic effects are obtained, so too it set out to prove that the title "poem" is no guarantee of poetic content.

The Dadaists who gave their attention to poetry began in a frame of mind similar to that of Tzara, wishing to break down time-honored preconceptions. So, though their methods were varied, their experimentation centered about this main concern. Some, like Philippe Soupault and Louis Aragon attacked the respectability of established poetry by inference, so to speak, in their use of banality and even obscenity. But though it is an easy matter to minimize the significance of their efforts, there is no denying their mockery of the poet's supposed need to communicate ideas, sensations, or emotions he feels must be shared. The danger is perhaps that, from the Dadaists' denial of poetry as they saw it practiced about them, may be inferred the very rejection of poetry. It is helpful, therefore, to glance at the diary of Hugo Ball who, as early as 1916, was writing phonetic poems based on sounds rather than meaningful words, with the purpose of "renouncing devastated language, rendered impossible by journalism." Dada poetry, as represented in Ball's phonetic experiments, does not stand for the abandonment of poetry, but reflects the conviction that we should "withdraw into the most profound alchemy of the word, and even abandon the word." [7] Only sound, Ball implies, remains uncontaminated by everyday use.

Dada, therefore, used shock tactics, and reserved for itself the most complete liberty. But not to the extent of so withdrawing into anarchy as to lose contact with society. Irresponsible the Dadaists' behavior evidently was; but it was deliberately so. Dada's refusal to submit to the obligations society would impose was a conscious and seriously motivated one, despite its apparent impertinence and frivolity. Nonsense had its point, mockery its target, as the Dada spirit impelled certain men to offer society a violent shock, believed necessary to release society from a complacency that marked a decline in sincere artistic response. Society must be detached from its preconceptions and its misconceptions. It must be taught new criteria, a new responsiveness. So, in poetry the Dadaists set out to destroy the stock response, and to condemn that type of verse which seeks to command respect simply by calling itself poetry. Thus the first step entailed questioning all that had come to be taken for granted.

To some it seems that this first step was also the last, that Dada never developed beyond this primary stage. While it is true that a number of Dadaists were content to confine their attention to immediate aims, the best among them were keenly conscious of a further effort remaining to be made. These appreciated that, if they could with relative ease prove their first point—their disapproval of poetry in its existing forms—they still had to persuade the public that it was possible to proceed to a further stage and demonstrate that poetry could be something different, something new.

Hans Arp was one of the limited number aware of deeper concerns than revolt for its own sake. He has reported in *On My Way* (1948) his attempts to replace old techniques with more efficacious ones, and recorded his urge to "create a new universe." He has told too of his increasing confidence in chance, which led him to conclude that the laws of chance are "the highest and deepest of laws, the law that rises from the fundament." His poetic methods—especially in his *Wolkenpumpe* poems in their stress upon chance—recall Tzara's proposals and foreshadow some of the techniques to be practiced only a few years later by the Surrealists.

In poetry, then, Dada's sense of disgust and of consequent mistrust brought a demand for a complete revision of values, expressed through a search for new methods. Consciously sensational at times, and even deliberately calculated to provoke ridicule, Dadaist poetry was nevertheless at its best fundamentally serious. For this reason, though Dada may not have made much immediate impact upon poetry, it was soon to make itself felt in notable measure in Surrealist poetry. Dada must be regarded as a historical necessity. While the century was still young, it represented the spirit of integral nonconformity, epitomizing—eventually at the price of its own extinction—the need for the *tabula rasa*. It demanded a revision of values to do away with the conditioned reflexes upon which the poetry of the day seemed to thrive. So the poetic practices of the Dadaist poets were indicative of wider concerns. The ultimate aim was to disturb society and upset its complacency. As Theo Van

Doesburg said, Art with a capital "A" must go—for Dada, announced Paul Dermée in his review *Z* (1920), "jeers atrociously at capital letters." Capitalization denotes consecration and confirms recognition by a social organization upon which Dada had declared war.

It must be conceded that Dada's nonconformity was of a character to attract more attention than the aims motivating it. And too many of the Dadaists were, like George Grosz,[8] content with rendering explicit their sense of difference from society, and saw no further than this. But this does not prevent Dadaist activities from assuming real pertinence, when viewed from a distance. Those for whom Dada is anti-art yet at the same time art seem to imagine they have discovered a paradox that reveals the Dadaists to be unfaithful to their own principles. The truth is that this paradox is of Dada's invention, as some consideration of Dadaist painting will show.

The Dadaists did all they could to attack academicism. So, in its most sensational form, Dadaist painting is eminently iconoclastic, like the *Dada Picture* executed by Francis Picabia. This characteristic work consists of a toy monkey nailed to a canvas bearing around its edges the words "Portrait de Cézanne," "Portrait de Rembrandt," "Portrait de Renoir," "Natures mortes." The choice of key figures from the official history of painting together with the suggestion, both verbal and visual, that they are in every way dead— grinning corpses like the monkey—typifies the immediate aims of Dada in painting. Through works like this, Dada's dismissal of the past was clearly established, as was the determination to refuse respect for recognized painters of established reputation. Nothing, Picabia and his friends suggested, can be gained by apeing the past. So if accepted masterpieces are accorded any attention, it must only be to discredit them. Destruction then is intentional, a necessary preliminary to the conquest of new freedom, unhindered by all that has been done in the past.

The iconoclasm of the Dadaist painter did not aim at dislodging respected idols for the pure joy of seeing them fall. Like the Dadaist poet, he questioned the dignity of the artistic process as it is generally understood. Some Dadaists voluntarily surrendered their share in this dignity when they abstained from signing their works, or signed one another's, or incorporated into their products ephemeral materials which would make their survival in a museum most unlikely. Dada's repeated reminder that art has no indisputable right to survive reflects a spirit of anti-conformity which found perfect expression in the collages it inspired.

The use of collage technique can be traced back to the eighteenth century. And just before the advent of Dada the Cubists had made collages having a function quite different from that which Dada was to reserve for them. In the Cubist collage the element of surprise introduced by the technique does not disguise the fact that what the artist has in mind is the production of an harmonious whole from disparate elements, seeking contrasts of texture and form, allowed to play their part only under the strictest control. If the Cubist collage incorporates nonpictorial elements, it is with a definite assimilative process in mind. In Dadaist collages, on the other hand, no such process is even attempted. The Dadaist chooses materials at random, and juxtaposes them without trying to establish or even hint at any relationship. Harmony as it is conventionally understood is sacrificed, not to say deliberately excluded, and the spectator is denied the comfort of detecting a rational or aesthetic relationship between the elements confronting him. Thus we witness the destruction of the systems of classification to which we have become accustomed by habit and education. A quality of devaluation gives such collages a scandalous quality. But we sense also an effort toward revaluation through an impression of a world in metamorphosis, that takes us beyond mere provocation to a glimpse of revelations made possible by the refusal to accept limitations so few of us are ready to question.

In the world the Dadaist creates with apparent negligence, may be recognized elements borrowed from our own

universe as well as those quite foreign to our experience.
Meanwhile the former are modelled and fashioned according
to laws quite unfamiliar to us. This is why to catalogue the
materials appearing in a Dadaist collage or forming a
Dadaist object, is already to start in the wrong direction.
The deceptive humility of the materials utilized communi-
cates to the spectator no feeling of reassurance or superi-
ority, because they are already taken out of the classifications to which the public is accustomed. Placed in new,
exciting relation to one another, a broken coat-hanger and a
piece of cork may still be identifiable as such—and much of
the impact of Dada would be lost if they had ceased to be
so—but are already reaching out for another identity of a
kind our world would be unable to assimilate and submit to
its laws. In this way, the Dadaist questions our right to put a
name to things and freeze them in immobility. The world of
the banal and the familiar give place to a new universe
where may be encountered unnameable objects conventional
language is incapable of describing, resistant to any attempt
to impose upon their meaning habitual limits.

It matters little whether the artist himself is fully aware
of what he has accomplished. It matters even less whether he
intends his creation as a joke or not. Indeed, two of the most
important lessons learned from Dada by Surrealism were
that jokes may be productive and that it is sometimes pref-
erable that the artist remain unaware of what he is producing, rather than submit to the temptation to interfere in a
way which may reduce the effective power of what he creates.

As is the case with some Dadaist poetry, certain Dadaist
collages and graphic works owe their origin to chance alone.
In his *Flucht aus der Zeit*, Ball tells how he, Tzara and Arp
worked with Picabia on an illustration for the third number
of the review *Dada*. Taking apart an old clock, they bathed
the detached pieces in ink, before pressing them at random
on a sheet of paper. In this deliberately mechanical process—foreshadowing, incidentally, Surrealist experimentation with automatism—the forms utilized were left, Ball
claims, entirely to chance, as was their arrangement upon

the paper. Though it is easy to mistrust the value of such experiments, one cannot deny how successfully here chance is allowed to usurp the role of artistic temperament, in a deliberately collective effort. Creative energy finds itself released by novel and intentionally revolutionary means, implementing both a new attitude toward art and a new relationship between the work of art and its creator. This relationship may be conveniently examined through a brief consideration of Marcel Duchamp's "ready mades."

Varied and fascinating as Duchamp's activities have been, he is no doubt generally known as the enigmatic creator of ready-mades, which we may best understand if we begin with a phrase from the diary Arp published in *transition* in 1932: "Dada wanted to change the perceptible world of man today into a pious, senseless world without reason." For according to Duchamp's own definition ready-mades "deny the possibility of defining art" and take away the technical jargon of art. Through his ready-mades Duchamp attacked the creative act itself, and the dignity with which this act is usually invested. So ready-mades are everyday objects raised to the status of artistic signification solely by the whim of the artist who has first chosen, then named his object. The creative art is consequently complete as soon as the choice has been made. The irony is complete when Duchamp, echoing Dermée's condemnation of capital letters, calls his bicycle wheel *Bicycle Wheel*, his snow shovel *Snow Shovel*.

Nowhere does Dada's militant use of nonsense more successfully find expression than in Duchamp's ready-mades, which require the spectator to reconsider the criteria by which artistic achievement is to be assessed. And Duchamp invited his public not simply to revise their standards, but to take a second look at the things about them, now liberated from utilitarian associations, thus exploring one of the paths to be taken during Surrealism's revolt against accepted reality.

The immediate effect of the ready-made was to offer a notable contribution to the subversive activity of Dada, in which many took a hand. Arp, for instance, devised numerous absurd objects, which he has since described in *On My Way*. Objects such as these and Duchamp's give substance to Max Ernst's affirmation: "Dada was a bomb." So did the celebrated Dada Manifestations.

The manifestation in Cologne, organized by Arp, Ernst, and Baargeld in 1920, was held in a glassed-in court, accessible only through a public urinal. The choice of locale marked an act of deliberate bad taste, calculated to exclude the dilettante, the gallery-goer who attends exhibitions not to see but to be seen. Dada's refusal to compromise with conventionality is reflected here, as is its determination to go its own way, to the accompaniment of insult and provocation.

The Dadaists knew perfectly well what they were doing when, in Paris, they announced that Charlie Chaplin would be present at one of their manifestations, or when they promised to have their heads shaved in public. They wilfully deceived their audience, and then added insult to injury by making it quite clear they had never intended to fulfil their promise. The public was cheated, and ridiculed too. But what is more they were made to understand that the Dadaists were ready to break the social pact presupposed by their invitations and promises.

It is significant that Richard Huelsenbeck, in a broadcast interview, has carefully distinguished between Dada and Dadaism. Dada represents the spirit. Dadaism is the movement which this spirit did inspire, but not always guide. Dada's self-conscious iconoclasm, fostered in a world torn by war, unrest and dissatisfaction, aimed to prepare for new beginnings. Dadaism, as evidenced in the conduct of its proponents, was often too involved in the processes of rejection and destruction to keep in view long-term ambitions. And this is in large measure why Dadaism very soon lost from sight the ultimate goal, falling into sterility and self-repetition.

Distinguishing therefore the spirit of Dada from the organized movement we know as Dadaism, one may better appreciate the important part played by Dada in the evolution of twentieth-century attitudes and preoccupations in art and literature. And the importance of Dada must be recognized even though it raised more problems than it solved. For these problems have proved to be among the most significant and compelling of our time. Dada posed fundamentally the question of honesty in art, just as it posed that of the function of art in society. It then took the logical step of drawing attention to the artist's relationship to his public, redefining in acutely pertinent terms the problem of artistic responsibility. This, in turn, led to consideration of the public's relation to art, and that of inspiration to artistic expression. In its early days especially, Dada represented a spirit of restless inquiry, indisputably alert and pertinent to its period. Thus, though the movement called Dadaism soon died, the spirit of Dada, transmuted and somewhat refined, dressed up certainly with more sophistication, continued to exert some of its influence through a new movement, founded—inevitably, it must now seem—by a former Dadaist. Surrealism learned from Dada more than a variety of attitudes and technical devices. It learned that revolt, before it is anything else, is a state of mind.

Yesterday in the Palais Royal Gardens was found the body of Dada. Suicide was presumed (for the wretch threatened from birth to end his days) when André Breton made a full confession.   Jacques Rigaut

In his book *L'Aventure Dada* Georges Hugnet divides the history of Dada into phases, with each of which he associates the name of a city. His method, which permits him to speak of Dada in New York as well as in Zurich, Cologne and Paris, has the merit of permitting him to stress differences of tone and rhythm, as he shows Dada asserting its influence, affirming its principles in various capitals. Though nothing would be gained by covering this ground once more, it is worth noting that in spreading outward from Zurich, Dada influence found the ground well prepared in France to accept the seed and ensure its germination.

The future Surrealist leader, André Breton, saw the first two numbers of the review *Dada* in the Paris apartment of Guillaume Apollinaire. But, according to Breton's own admission, he did not become really enthusiastic about Dada until he read Tzara's 1918 manifesto, reproduced in the

third number of *Dada.* This document Breton judged to be
"violently explosive." [1]

At first glance, however, Tzara's message would not seem
to have held much attraction for Breton. While Tzara called
vehemently for a break with standard forms of art and with
logic, and insisted upon "a great negative task to be accomplished," Breton in his early years had found a model in
Stéphane Mallarmé, and in Paul Valéry, whose insistence
upon formal perfection and order was diametrically opposed
to the ideas Tzara was promulgating. As a young man
Breton had even contributed verses to the review *La Phal-
ange,* which patently continued the traditions of Symbolism.
Indeed it seems very possible the message of Dada would
have held little meaning for André Breton, had he not
so very recently been subjected to first-hand experience of a
world at war.

There were some poets—and Apollinaire was one of
them—who derived aesthetic satisfaction from certain aspects of war, which they welcomed more or less consciously.
Others, including Breton, could bear the thought of war's
destruction and waste only so long as they retained the belief
that it must bring benefits eventually, that the world could
be a better place afterwards. This is to say that Breton was
destined to be one of those bitterly disappointed by the peace
that came in 1918. A sense of estrangement felt in wartime
by the soldiers returning from the front—admirably evoked
by Henri Barbusse in *Le Feu*—was a common enough experience. But the difficulties of peacetime rehabilitation proved
all the more complex in a man of Breton's sensibility and
intelligence who perceived that demobilization brought not
a solution to existing problems but a whole series of new
ones. Thus we find Breton relating in *Entretiens* how he
came to feel cheated by society. Even before his release
from the Army, he had begun to realize that, for him, there
could be no return to former positions and attitudes. He had
discovered in himself a new critical awareness, imposing
the conclusion that it would be impossible to come to terms
once more with a world that had learned nothing from the

atrocious misadventure of the war which had interrupted his own medical studies, and cut him off from his former self.

Evidently, disruption in established habits of thought had made Breton especially responsive to the influence exerted upon his outlook on life by a strange personality encountered in Nantes in 1916: Jacques Vaché. Vaché, who was to take his own life when only twenty-three, impressed Breton as "a sort of Des Esseintes of action." His attitudes were to act as a kind of catylist upon Breton's half-formulated sense of revolt. They led Breton to liken him to the hero of Huysmans' novel *A Rebours*. Vaché's contribution to the lore of Surrealism was not literary, as he produced nothing beyond a series of letters—most of them addressed to Breton—in which we catch an echo of his strange detachment and the special kind of humor that he himself called "umour" and defined as a sense of "the theatrical (and joyless) inutility of everything. WHEN ONE KNOWS." But Vaché's intransigent iconoclasm exercised a compelling fascination for Breton, who has spoken in *Entretiens* of his "principle of total insubordination" undermining the world. "But for him," Breton has declared, "I would be a poet"—a poet, it goes without saying, of the type he was aspiring to be before the war obliged him to revise his ideas. Returning to civilian life permanently marked in his outlook by contact with Vaché, to whom he was to refer in his *Manifesto of Surrealism* as "Surrealist in me," Breton was to feel even more strongly that sense of dissatisfaction and restlessness this contact had fostered in him. He was now ready for new departures.

In *Entretiens* Breton has admitted to having been more or less ignorant, before 1914, of the latest developments in art and literature: Cubism and Futurism. Though he does not say so, it seems clear that this ignorance was not entirely attributable to inexperience. He had not at that time received the shock to his preconceptions that the next few years were to bring. His war service, though, left him in a frame of mind suited to respond readily to certain trends that had earlier escaped his attention. He was now ready to recognize in Apollinaire a poet of supreme significance.

This is not the place to discuss the prestige attaching in Surrealism to the name of Apollinaire.[2] But we may note how Breton speaks of him in *Entretiens*. Meeting Apollinaire for the first time in 1916, Breton revered in him the poet of "La Chanson du Mal Aimé," of "Zone," of "L'Emigrant de Landor Road," and "Le Musicien de Saint-Merry," the champion of the *poème-événement,* that is "the apostle of that conception which demands of every new poem that it be a total recasting of its author's means, that it seek adventure for itself outside defined paths, scornful of gains already made." Like Rimbaud, who was at this time attracting more and more attention among those later to become Breton's friends in Surrealism, Apollinaire was the poet-*seer*. Both Breton and Philippe Soupault (who later collaborated with him on the first specifically Surrealist texts, *Les Champs magnétiques*) regarded Apollinaire as a seer,[3] and their agreement on this point was to be one of their earliest links. As the example of Vaché had already done for Breton, Appollinaire's celebrated article "L'Esprit nouveau et les Poètes" seemed to give Soupault's feeling of revolt both purpose and direction in its assertion: "The divine eyes of life and imagination give full scope to an entirely new poetic activity." [4]

For Breton was not alone in the sentiments of which he speaks in *Entretiens*. He found kindred spirits: first Soupault, then Louis Aragon. Soupault has spoken in an article for *Réalités* of what united them at this time: "We were all three like explorers setting out to discover the literary world, but explorers who judged with severity the fauna of arts and letters." At this point—thanks to another young man who now joined the group, Théodore Fraenkel—the future Surrealists discovered another figure who was soon to take his place in their calendar of saints: Alfred Jarry, whose explosive humor did much to widen the gap between the present and the past, and pose the problem of the future with even greater urgency.

The sense of unity of which Soupault has spoken was soon to find practical expression when he, Breton, and Aragon founded a review entitled *Littérature*. Its first number appeared in 1918. It was *Littérature* which became instrumental in bringing to the attention of the Dadaists in Zurich the efforts of the growing group of discontented ex-service intellectuals in France. But at first the review aimed at a sort of synthesis. The editors indicated this by their retention of certain notable figures of an earlier generation. So the list of contributors including André Gide, Paul Valéry, Léon-Paul Fargue, André Salmon, Pierre Reverdy and Blaise Cendrars, and even Pierre Morand, Jean Giraudoux and Pierre Drieu La Rochelle. But what strikes the reader of *Littérature* today is the contribution made by Breton, by Soupault, by Aragon, and by a newcomer, Paul Eluard. So, in the oddly mixed early numbers, Lautréamont's *Poésies* (copied by Breton from the only extant copy, in the Bibliothèque Nationale), Jacques Vaché's *Lettres de Guerre*, and articles on Raymond Roussel stand out noticeably. Finally, the attempt to combine the revolutionary with the conventional was deemed a failure. Looking back on this period, Breton has commented in *Entretiens:* "What good was there in attempting any longer this impossible synthesis of elements which could be brought together in a way that satisfied the sense of quality, but would never have anything to do with one another?" *Littérature* was fast becoming an anthology. And Breton—eager to communicate the message he had begun to learn from Vaché—soon realized that an anthology cannot express a programme, however vaguely formulated, unless the choice of its elements be submitted to the strictest control.

At this point Dada's impact brought results which seemed especially welcome. Already out of sympathy with contemporary forms of literary activity, Breton and his friends were quite prepared to take advantage of Dada's invitation to do away with all restraints. Hausmann's declaration in *Dada est plus que Dada* appeared to be quite a programme in itself: "Dada is the kick in the kidneys and the slap in the face for those virtuous apprentices of civilization." If we recall that Aragon has spoken in his *L'Homme communiste* of the Paris group's passionate search, their bursting desire to tear down pretence wherever they found it, to react against complacency and to make the fullest demands upon themselves as well as upon society, it is not surprising that when, in 1919, Tzara arrived in Paris to organize Dadaist activities there, he was acclaimed by an enthusiastic and determined group of young men, already eager to give of their best in the cause of Dada.

Now the uncompromising tone of Dadaist pronouncements in Zurich found resounding echo in Paris. Generally-accepted principles, like morality and good taste, were rejected. Meanwhile the negative message of Dada was reiterated in new manifestoes, and in public manifestations.

The first Dada manifestation held in Paris was organized under the auspices of *Littérature,* on January 23, 1920. Very soon articles by Tzara and Picabia were appearing in *Littérature,* which devoted a number in May 1920 entirely to Dada, carrying "Twenty-Three Manifestoes of the Dada Movement," to which Aragon, Breton and Soupault all contributed. Meanwhile public Dada shows continued, culminating in the celebrated "Dada Festival" held in the eminently respectable Salle Gaveau—a show at which the audience was sufficiently incensed to bombard the performers with beef steaks.

In June of the same year a permanent exhibition of Dada was established at the Galerie Montaigne, opened to the accompaniment of a suitable manifestation. As usual, the names of Aragon, Soupault and Eluard appeared on the invitation announcing the exhibition. But that of Breton was absent. He had declined to participate for reasons made public in an article, "Pour Dada," published the following year, and reprinted in his *Les Pas perdus* (1924).

After explaining the common ground which existed between himself and those who still placed their confidence in Dada, Breton added, "My friends Philippe Soupault and Paul Eluard will not contradict me if I say we have never regarded 'Dada' as anything but a rough image of a state of mind that it by no means helped to create." It seemed to Breton, therefore, as he watched the way Dadaism was taking, that the end had been lost from sight, thanks to the energy and enthusiasm with which immediate means were being exploited. Under Tzara's leadership, the movement deriving from Dada was becoming fixed in a set of pre-scribed attitudes and standard gestures, doomed, it ap-peared to Breton, to sterility. It was time, if not to stop, then to adopt a new approach.

Dadaism had lost the spontaneity that had been its chief attraction for Breton and his French associates. It was, in fact, falling into the same errors as those that had vitiated academic art and traditional literary approaches, ceasing to fulfill its destiny as a stimulant. Its moral force was being sapped by repetition and the absence of variation: it was, in Breton's phrase, "marking time."

A measure of Dadaism's failure to progress in its exist-ing form was, to Breton, the publication in *La Nouvelle Re-vue française* of an article by its editor entitled "Reconnais-sance à Dada." That gratitude towards Dada should be ex-pressed in such a respectable periodical was indeed a sign of the times. For Breton, this marked the collapse of what amounted to orthodox Dadaism, which had unaccountably drifted into literary consecration. It was the end of the line Dadaism had been traveling, up to the time of Breton's withdrawal. A radical change in direction would be neces-sary before he could consent to give it confidence once again.

The spectacle of Dada, the very negation of orthodoxy, taking its place in literature was warning enough. In con-junction with Aragon, Breton sought to give Dadaism new orientation, proposing "a radical renewal of means, for the pursuit of the same aims through absolutely different chan-nels." Significant among their efforts were visits they planned to various sites in Paris. Organized on the tourist pattern, these proposed visits would reveal a characteristic tone of Dada mockery, evidenced in the choice of buildings to be examined: the church of St. Julien le Pauvre, the Lycée

Janson de Sailly, the Morgue, the Louvre, St. Lazare Station. But they were more important as an attempt to establish once more some contact with a public the habitual Dadaist methods were fast alienating. It is worth noting, in the circumstances, that only one visit actually took place before the project failed. Even so, this proposal reflects the original seriousness of Dada, from which Tzara and his companions were wandering. This seriousness is even more noticeable in Breton's idea of conducting a public trial of Maurice Barrès.

Barrès was selected as the personification of respectable and respected conformism: the writer who, in Breton's view, had come to terms with society at the price of his own integrity. Many of those who attended the public hearing, to find Barrès represented by a tailor's dummy, must have expected the same amalgam of buffoonery and abuse to which recent Dadaist shows in Paris had accustomed them. But they soon discovered that Breton, who had cast himself in the role of judge, was proposing to treat the whole matter with unexpected gravity. So the trial was the occasion of a public display of the growing hostility between Breton and Tzara, who found himself rebuked for frivolity. Breton's summation, after Aragon—a defense council, as it happened—had demanded the death penalty, is worth citing in full: "Dada, judging the time has come to endow its negative spirit with executive powers, and determined above all to exercise these powers against those who threaten its dictatorship, is beginning, as of this date, to take appropriate measures. Believing that a given man who, in a given period, is capable of solving certain problems is guilty if, whether from a desire for tranquillity, or from a need for outward show of action, or from self-kleptomania, or for moral reasons, he renounces that which is unique in himself, if he agrees with those who maintain that without experience of life and awareness of its responsibilities, there can be no more possession of oneself, if he interferes with whatever revolutionary power may reside in the activity of those who might be tempted to learn from his first lesson; Dada accuses Maurice Barrès of offense against the security of the spirit."

For the first time the resounding voice of André Breton makes itself heard with its characteristic tone. And the contrast with Tzara's attitude becomes immediately clear. The growing sense of irresponsibility with which Tzara had infected the Dadaists is replaced by a new sense of purpose which, under Breton's guidance, will mark the Surrealists. This is what makes Breton's brief fidelity to Dadaism so interesting, for those seeking to follow out the emergence of Surrealist principles. Tzara, whom Huelsenbeck has called "the journalistic brain of Dada," continued to give his attention to publicity and propaganda. But Breton was already announcing in 1921—the year of the Barrès trial—"The moral question preoccupies me."

Dada's destructive work had been necessary, Breton would agree, to prepare for the rehumanization of literature and art. He came to feel concern only when he sensed the reluctance of many of his companions to take matters further. For this reason, the Barrès trial represented an effort to recall Dadaism to its essentially serious task of questioning and reforming accepted attitudes. It was because he had become convinced that this was the task Dada must always face that Breton had joined the movement, in a mood of hope. Dada had seemed to offer a possible outlet for aspirations and energies that society was reducing to frustration. It proposed a line of conduct when nothing else seemed to hold any promise. But Breton quite soon came to understand that the Dadaism of Tzara could take him only a limited distance along the road he wished to travel. In the light of events, it is evident that he demanded more than Dadaism could give him. For him, the essential problem was summed up in the question given prominence in his "Confession dédaigneuse," which he reprinted in *Les Pas perdus:* "How to accept the unacceptable human condition?" Despite early optimism, Breton was not slow to discover that Dadaism seemed unlikely to solve this question. Within the Dadaist group, he found himself no nearer "escaping so far as possible from the human type from which we all derive."

In 1922, Breton conceived an International Congress for the Determination of Directives and the Defense of the Modern Spirit. This he wished to organize with the participation of certain non-Dadaists. Violently opposed by Tzara, however, this Paris Congress finally collapsed, its failure marking Breton's definitive withdrawal from Dadaism. Within two years he had published his *Manifesto of Surrealism,* thus publicly demonstrating his break with Dada.

In 1919, Breton has explained in his *Entretiens,* Tzara was awaited in Paris "like a messiah." By 1924, Breton had become his own messiah, and was already gathering about him his disciples. The change of viewpoint is startling, at first glance. A closer examination reveals it to have been effected with much less dramatic suddenness than a simple comparison of dates would seem to imply.

Breton's association with Dadaism had developed in him an independence of mind, a need for complete liberty, and a conviction that success depends upon individual effort. Basically, however, Dadaism had done little more than strengthen in him the determination to continue his search in the face of society, even though he was not yet sure where this search would lead. Neither he nor those who lent him support had definite ideas about what they wished to accomplish. If all would agree that Dada had helped to clarify issues to a considerable extent, they would have been hard put to it, between 1921 and 1924, to say what the next step must be.

This is not to say that there was no evidence as yet of a half-conscious groping for something more than Dada had to offer. In fact such evidence was present, in part, in *Littérature.* As early as October 1919 *Littérature* had published the first part of *Les Champs magnétiques,* written in collaboration by Breton and Philippe Soupault and recognized as the first specifically Surrealist text. The future

Surrealists, then, did not have to wait until Dada had ceased to hold their attention before they followed lines of experimentation later to become increasingly important for them. Already Eluard was composing some of the texts to be published in 1926 under the title *Les Dessous d'une Vie, ou la Pyramide humaine.* In collaboration with Max Ernst, he was working on *Les Malheurs des Immortels,* to appear in 1922. Meanwhile Breton was already exploring techniques which culminated in *Poisson soluble,* published in 1924 in conjunction with the *Manifesto of Surrealism.*

Examples like these may be cited without any suggestion being made that the full implications of certain techniques, later characteristic of Surrealism, were immediately apparent to men not yet calling themselves Surrealists. On the contrary, it is the distinction of the first *Manifesto* that it gave meaning to a varied and only loosely related body of material, submitting it to a revealing coherence. The *Manifesto* permitted recognition of Surrealist characteristics in pictorial as well as literary products, created in many cases by artists who, like Max Ernst, still regarded themselves as supporters of Dadaism. This sort of overlapping in the transition from Dadaism to Surrealism is a phenomenon of notable interest, permitting us to appreciate that the famous *Manifesto* did not appear unannounced. It makes clear also that Breton's text was addressed, if not to a well-defined group of young men, then to quite a considerable number of individuals—many of them publicly acknowledged in the *Manifesto* itself—who were undoubtedly prepared for its message, for that sense of unified purpose it offered them, and for the welcome cohesion it gave their aspirations.

But just as Surrealism's break with Dadaism was less sudden than might have been expected, so it was also less violent. Not that Surrealism was simply Dadaism under a new flag and a new leader. But Surrealism owed so much to Dada—even in its conscious reaction against Dadaism—as to be incomprehensible in many of its aspects if it is not understood that, despite their conviction that Dadaism had served its purpose, the Surrealists, though not precisely continuing Dadaism, took from it what they deemed useful to their purpose.

In *Donner à Voir* (1939), Eluard wrote, "In February 1917, the Surrealist painter Max Ernst and I were at the front, hardly a kilometre from one another. The German gunner Max Ernst was shelling the trenches where I, a French infantryman, was on guard. Three years later, we were the best of friends and we have fought together relentlessly since, for the same cause, that of the total emancipation of man." By 1920 both Eluard and Ernst were Dadaists. Yet when they finally rallied to Surrealism neither found it necessary to give up his belief in the prime need for total emancipation. The desire for complete freedom, basic to Dadaist attitudes, remains characteristic for all who evolved toward Surrealism, just as it distinguished, later, those Surrealists who had never been associated with Dadaism. In this respect, Surrealism is a prolongation of Dadaism in its most productive mood, a continued plea for liberation. The *Manifesto of Surrealism* proudly proclaimed Surrealism to be "our absolute nonconformism," evidently to be developed at the expense of the claims society would impose upon the individual.

It is noteworthy, however, that in reiterating the basic Dada principle of revolt, the Surrealists have taken care to avoid pitfalls to which Dadaism led. When, more than twenty years after his first manifesto, Breton published *Arcane 17* (1944) and defined *liberty* "by opposition to all the forms of servitude and restraint," he was at pains to indicate the weaknesses of his own definition. Seen this way, liberty is presented as a *state*—as Breton says: "that is, in immobility." But the whole of human experience, we are assured, demonstrates that "this immobility ensures its immediate ruin." Showing he had learned his lesson from Dadaism, Breton now prefers to define liberty as "a *living force* ensuring a continual progression."

Nevertheless, the essential point remains the same. The Surrealists reaffirm the Dadaists' concern for the value and role of human destiny within the social and cultural framework of the modern world, holding society responsible for aggravating, if not for creating, man's unhappy condition. So many of the organizations and conventions of the world of today receive the same bitter mockery from Surrealism as from Dada. Through Pierre Mabille's book *Le Merveilleux* (1946), the Surrealists speak of society as "a cultivated and stratified scab, which tends to separate more and more seriously the inner fire of our being from the universe which surrounds it." This is to say that the unqualified opposition offered by Dadaism to society assumes in Surrealism a grave significance, the public statements which evidence the Surrealists' differences with society representing, after the undifferentiated condemnation of Dada, a new call to order.

The clearly subversive attitude of Surrealism was soon to find unequivocal expression through a series of open letters, that began to appear soon after the *Manifesto,* in Surrealism's first review, *La Révolution surréaliste,* founded in 1924. Distinctive among these, and apparently indicating a departure from Dadaism, was the letter addressed to the Pope, which for the first time made public the Surrealists' rejection of Christianity. This letter has been followed by so much proof of detestation for Christian religion that we must pause to examine its significance.

Surrealism has been adamantly opposed to Christianity for at least two reasons, the first of which shows that the Surrealists have not moved so far from Dadaism as might be thought. Victor Crastre summed it up in the sixth number of *La Révolution surréaliste,* in 1926: "God and society are one and the same thing." Surrealism's anti-Christian attitude is, then, a corollary of its refusal to be bound by the restrictions society imposes. Thus far, at least, Surrealism's attitude must be viewed as an extension of Dada. We are taken a step further, though, by Crastre's words: "It is only beyond God that we can create a new world." Here is the source of the continued vitality of Surrealism's denial of orthodox religion: the belief expressed with convenient clarity by Maxime Alexandre in the opening number of the second

Surrealist review, *Le Surréalisme au service de la Révolution* (1930) : "The religious spirit is that body of sentiments and ideas which tend to maintain man a prisoner of himself and of other men." The point is important for an accurate impression of Surrealism and what it aspires to achieve. Antagonism to Christianity is not, and could not be, confined to the early days of Surrealist activity, when it might seem to have been attributable to a variety of causes, not the least of them being youthful exuberance. So far as the Surrealists are concerned, it is not a matter of echoing much that has been said before. Instead, they have taken the logical step imposed upon them by their programme of integral revolt. The fundamental difference between Surrealism and Christianity is that the latter asks us to believe salvation to be the prerogative of an agency outside man, whereas the Surrealists have always remained persuaded that it is man's own concern, his own responsibility, to be won by his own efforts.

"We are not waiting for Godot," declared Ado Kyrou in a number of the Surrealist review, *Médium*. Rejecting the religious overtones of Beckett's play, the Surrealists reject at the same time the limitations they feel in religious sentiment, joining with Breton in this essential ambition: "We want, we will have the *beyond* in our time."

Anyone sharing this ambition, in whatever form, is accorded the support of the Surrealist group. So the Surrealist open letter to directors of insane asylums declared in 1925: "We cannot admit the hindrance of the free development of human ideas and acts." Surrealism's attitude towards insanity will call for some comment later. It is enough, here, to note how the vindication of total liberty leads the Surrealists to embrace the cause even of those society believes incapable of taking full advantage of liberty. In fact their right to freedom appears particularly important to the group who wrote in an open letter to the rectors of European universities: "In the narrow cisterns you call 'thought,' spiritual rays rot like a straw." By what right, they asked in 1926, did the universities claim to "canalize intelligence"? It is "the unlimited capacity for *refusal*," Breton explained almost ten years later in his *Position politique du Surréalisme* (1935), that is "the whole secret of humanity's movement forward."

From the very beginning, Surrealism has regarded liberty as man's most precious possession, "opposing," in Breton's phrase, "with an irreducible 'no' all disciplinary formulae." So to undermine society continues to be one of the primary aims of the Surrealists, as it had been for the Dadaists. Breton's *Position politique du Surréalisme* dismissed as meaningless for Surrealism the words *patrie*, *justice*, and *devoir*, as these are understood within the narrow limits of nationalism. And the Surrealists have cited Italy's invasion of Ethiopia, the war in Spain, Japan's invasion of China as one decade's evidence of the baneful effects of nationalism, hiding behind words like "democracy" and "liberty."

Recognizing a certain community of aim with Marxism, the Surrealists were not slow to side with Communism against bourgeois society. Within a year of the appearance of the *Manifesto of Surrealism* Breton's tract *Légitime Défense* proclaimed in September 1926 the Surrealists' adhesion to the Communist programme, which was accepted, it is true, only as "a minimum programme." Certain hesitations—especially from the Communist side, which mistrusted the Surrealists for their bourgeois origins—and even disagreements seemed to have been resolved when the Surrealists, discontinuing their first review, baptized its successor *Le Surréalisme au service de la Révolution*. As suspicious as the society from which the Surrealists were careful to dissociate themselves and disturbed by a lack of seriousness in these young men, the Communists demanded more than assurances of solidarity. They required complete dedication to the cause of Marxist revolution. But when Aragon agreed to these terms, and entered the Communist Party, he and those who followed his example were expelled from the Surrealist group. Surrealism's severance from Communism was finally confirmed by a tract published in

1935 under the title *Du Temps que les Surréalistes avaient raison,* signed by twenty-six Surrealists headed by Breton.

After a moment of initial enthusiasm that guided them towards Marxism, it became clear to the Surrealists that they had been attracted to Communism solely as to a revolutionary *state.* The long-term aims of Communism—the replacement of one form of social organization with another—could hold no lasting interest for them. So their momentary alignment with the Communists must now appear inevitably destined to fail.[5] Breton and his companions discovered they had to choose between the cause of the Party and the cause to which they had dedicated themselves. Integral liberty, they learned, must begin with individual liberty. So while appreciating that they and Communism were following parallel routes, they reserved the right to branch off whenever it suited them, that is when they felt impelled to do so to remain faithful to their deepest convictions. So far as the Surrealist is concerned, nothing must be permitted to divert man from his main preoccupation: the search for and revelation of the surreal—a search in which social revolution is but the first, if essential step.

Surrealism finds its aggressiveness in a vitality drawing stimulus from the very opposition it provokes in an unsympathetic public. But its aggressiveness, so close on the surface to that of Dada, is the reflection of a profound concern, and the necessity to keep certain issues well in view. So Surrealist scandal is the outward expression of a persistent desire for a change long overdue. If the Surrealists advocate liberty, it is upon the understanding that man will turn it to account. Working always for what Breton has called "the greater liberation of the mind," the Surrealists are not content to pursue freedom solely in political directions. Surrealism represents for them a quest which leads to the use of certain means of investigation, reflecting a fundamental need to explore and to discover. Conceiving Surrealism as essentially a process by which man contrives to bring himself to the point where, in Breton's phrase, the mind has only to "make the final leap," the Surrealists have given much attention to the ways in which this process may be set in motion. Their discussion of this question by no means relieves the individual of the necessity to advance as far as he can along the road that promises most. So it is here that individual liberty assumes importance, constituting as it does the premise from which the confidence of Surrealism grows. In Surrealism, each must tread for himself the path of total comprehension, benefiting along the way from the signposts erected by those who have preceded him, but resisting the temptation to wait by the wayside when he has reached the point beyond which no one appears to have advanced. Breton's second Surrealist Manifesto speaks then of "a highly important reconnoissance" which each must undertake on his own account if he is to advance along this path. But what do Breton's words mean?

Approaching the published statements of Surrealism with this question in mind, one is impressed by the fact that no clear-cut reply has so far been offered. In comparison with the care taken to make plain the revolutionary ethos of Surrealism, concrete proposals on this point are difficult to find. Indeed, it becomes increasingly evident that the Surrealists have remained notably vague about their ultimate aims. The high-sounding phrases—as Breton's show—recur often enough. But this does not compensate for a remarkable degree of indecisiveness. So, the cover of the first number of *La Révolution surréaliste* bears the inscription: "We must arrive at a new declaration of the rights of man." But there is no indication of the possible character of these rights. Opening the cover we may read: "Surrealism does not offer itself as setting out a doctrine. Certain ideas that at present serve to support it do nothing to prejudice its later development. This first number of *La Révolution surréaliste* does not therefore present any final revelation. . . . We must await the future." In the event, however, the future brought little clarification, so that we find the first number of the review *NEON* which the Surrealists published in 1948 announcing: "We wish to be prisms fully reflecting all lights, especially those still unknown to us."

The pattern is so consistent that it imposes the conclusion that we are faced not so much with indecision or even with reluctance, but with a definite refusal beyond a certain stage to specify intentions. Its explanation seems to have been offered quite early in Surrealism's active period by Louis Aragon, discussing the recently opened Office for Surrealist Research: "We are working at a task that is enigmatic even to us." Such a task admits of no precise limits, even limits of its own devising. An openness of mind, the readiness to give himself up to any invitation or temptation promising to enrich his experience—these are the distinguishing marks of the true Surrealist. Thanks to its reluctance to impose restrictions upon its ambitions, Surrealism has remained a tantalizing potentiality to be realized only by opposition to what Breton has called "the constraints that weigh upon supervised thought." For it is only then that we can hope to agree with Breton's famous declaration, borrowed from his *Second Manifesto of Surrealism* (1930) : "Everything leads us to believe there exists a certain point in the mind in which life and death, real and imaginary, past and future, communicable and incommunicable, high and low cease to be perceived as contradictions." Here is the reward for escaping from the constraints of which Breton speaks. For this reason Surrealism, Breton affirms, has no other motive than "the hope of determining this point."

The prevailing sense of optimism underlying the Surrealists' statements of the last forty years gives meaning to Breton's claim that "to attribute to Surrealism a solely destructive or constructive meaning would be absurd." The point upon which his preoccupations focus is that at which construction and destruction become one. This is what he meant when he spoke in his second manifesto of Surrealism's tendency to provoke "*a crisis of consciousness* of the most general kind."

To characterize this crisis one can do no better than consider the two poles of experience recognized in Surrealism: the *eternal* and the *present*. For Breton, writing in *View* in August 1941, the former is represented by "the mind at grips with the human condition," while the latter is "the mind as witness of its own movement." The best Surrealist art, therefore, makes the public aware of this polarity, and places us in relation to it, through our reaction both to what Breton calls its manifest content and to its latent content. An especially interesting evolution in Breton's attitude is perceptible here. A sense of the dichotomy of which he speaks had already begun to dominate his thought before he abandoned Dadaism. But, with the clarification of Surrealism, it ceased to be a tragic one for him. For Surrealism is not simply the recognition of two poles of existence; it represents an attempt to effect their reconciliation. Thus we find Breton, interviewed for the *Correa Literario* in 1950, stressing that Surrealism has proposed to do nothing less than "enable the mind to leap the barrier set up for it by the antinomies of reason and dreaming, reason and madness, feeling and representation, etc., which constitute the major obstacle in western thought."

Surrealism's basic optimism is reflected in this ambition, and confirmed in the interview Breton gave *Le Littéraire* in October 1948, in which he discussed Surrealism's differences with Albert Camus. He remarked of the Surrealists, "They do not regard as incurable the 'fracture' observed by Camus between the Universe and the human mind." The Surrealists take their stand upon the conviction that man and the universe are not irreconcilable, without, for all that, minimizing or even trying to explain away the barrier opposing reconciliation. Just as nothing can be gained by waiting to pass into another form of existence—or another form of social organization—to find release from the tribulations of this world, so, Surrealism teaches, we gain nothing by turning our backs upon life. Man must seek and find his freedom now; he must establish means to bring into his experience, and into that of others, a sense of discovery, revelation and conquest, which Surrealism claims can come only from within man himself.

SURREALISM AND THE ARTS 3

*Surrealism is not a direction or a movement
in Art, it is a permanent state of the soul.*

Wilhelm Freddie

The painter Wilhelm Freddie is far from being alone in
considering Surrealism less as an artistic method than as a
state of the soul. The novelist Philippe Soupault, looking
back upon his days as a Surrealist, commented in a radio
interview, "I believe that when you are a Surrealist, you
can't be anything else.—It's a spirit, *un état d'esprit*." Remarks like these only confirm what we have already noticed:
in active Surrealism, the stress is upon life and thought, not
upon literature and language. The consequences of this emphasis must now be considered in relation to Surrealist
expression through painting and poetry.

During his radio interview, Soupault defined Surrealism
as "a sort of spiritual discovery." In doing so, he evidently
placed matters on a different footing from that which au-
thorized his remark cited a moment ago. Turning from Surrealism as a state of mind, Soupault was now concerned with
Surrealism as an activity, as action. It is therefore unfortu-
nate that no convenient terminology exists which would

permit the distinction between the state of mind and the activity of Surrealism, as we may distinguish between Dada and Dadaism. For such a distinction merits attention, since no valid examination of the technical devices characterizing Surrealist activity can be attempted until it has been established to what degree the Surrealist state of mind conditions this activity and the choice of these devices.

To make such a distinction when Surrealism is under discussion is particularly important. Acquaintance with certain types of Surrealist painting—the pictures of Dali come instantly to mind—to say nothing of the insidious process of popularization which Surrealism, despite its austerity, has not escaped, this has only too easily left the impression in the minds of many that Surrealist art and literature is no more than the exercise of a fairly limited number of techniques. Needless to say, these have lost some of their effectiveness—which, for some people, was confined in any case to their novelty—as they have become more familiar, and more widely imitated. The result is a series of erroneous conclusions that now stand between us and the comprehension of the true character of Surrealist art. Because this process of estrangement has proceeded furthest where pictorial Surrealism is concerned, it will prove particularly instructive to approach this question from the aspect of painting.

There is ample evidence of the complexity of the problem facing anyone wishing to arrive at a satisfactory but succinct definition of Surrealism. Although we are reminded that the term "surrealist" was first used by Apollinaire, his use of the adjective for his play *Les Mamelles de Tirésias* (1918) exercised no effective control over the meaning the Surrealists were to attach to it. And the passage of time has not rendered the task of definition any easier. All it has done is make one appreciate how summary explanations have the effect of over-simplifying issues. But the whole question has become complicated by a fact which soon strikes anyone who gives it serious attention. This is the marked difference to be observed between the way the Surrealists write of Surrealist painting, and the way art critics have written of it. It is consequently especially important to discover why such a disparity exists, and to establish why the pronouncements we owe to the Surrealists are more relevant than those made by outsiders.

It goes without saying that those Surrealists who have written and continue to write about painting are engaging, whether deliberately or not, in a form of propaganda. But this fact alone is insufficient to account for the widely differing estimates of the achievement of Surrealist painting, and would do little to recommend their opinion to us. One instance should suffice to indicate the complexity of the problem to be faced at this point.

In *Art News and Review* Lawrence Alloway asked on March 6, 1960: "Is Paul Jenkins a Surrealist?" It appears he is. He does not know it; neither do the Surrealists. But Alloway is confident: "Jenkins has declared that American abstract painting is 'not surreal' and has pointed to a lack of the 'obscure poetic resemblances' which are central to Surrealism. But his own work, both his technique and imagery, stays closer to Surrealism than most American painters would want to do now that the 1940s are over. His work shows an unbroken lyrical line back to Wols, as well as a personal penchant for exotic imagery. . . . His technique can also be linked with decalcomania by Dominguez and others." If this is not enough to classify Jenkins beyond doubt, then Alloway believes he has only to remind his readers that the painter has found in science "a source of wonder in nature useful to the artist," and the conclusion is then apparently inevitable: "Subjectivized science, as it has analogies with the dynamics of a painting process, is one more reason for typing Jenkins as, basically, a Surrealist." Even the tardy caution of the last phrase does little to repair the damage done by such glib type-casting, supported by equally glib generalizations, all of which are representative of a fundamentally unhelpful attitude of mind, having for effect the reduction of Surrealist painting to a set of techniques. Alloway, noticeably, fails even to mention the function the methods he identifies are supposed to serve, reducing the criticism of Surrealist art to a conditioned reflex.

One can easily see what results. Surrealist painting is attacked time and again both for its subject matter and for its techniques. In the form taken by these attacks can be seen only the extension of the process of misrepresentation we have just watched beginning to develop. Considered against the changing background of twentieth-century art in Western Europe, Surrealism can quite easily be interpreted as a retrograde step. To those who appreciate the efforts of Cubism to rescue painting from the consequences of mere representational treatment and who admire its attempt to offer the artist the opportunity to reorganize reality and submit it to patterns of his own choosing, Surrealism's return—in the early years especially—to a sometimes photographic realism must seem disappointing indeed. As if this were not enough cause for complaint, the Surrealists, apparently content to throw away the hard-earned advantages Cubism had brought, are seen as painters of *trompe-l'œil* exactitude, anecdotal artists with literary pretensions clearly reflected in their elaborate titles, to say nothing of their use of phrases and poems in their canvases. Meanwhile, in using humor these painters question the basic seriousness of art, so becoming even more suspect. And their patent exploitation of eroticism stands in defiance of standard morality, making them particularly vulnerable to attack.

So one of the basic impulses prompting antagonism toward Surrealist painting comes to light. For Frederick S. Wright, "Surrealism has the air of novelty, rather than the newness of creation, a way of astonishing by changing the subject." [1] Behind Wright's criticism is to be recognized the inference that, once the initial shock of a Surrealist picture has made its effect, the spectator feels cheated. There results a sense of grievance, most often vented in the form of criticism of the painter's technique. Thus, Pierre Schneider gibes: "The apocalyptic visions of Magritte or Tanguy are painted in the worst academic manner." [2] And in *Cobalto* (1948), Bernard Dorival politely chides Surrealism for "plastic indigence."

Others have been less restrained. Hugh Philip has put his sense of dissatisfaction more aggressively: "Frankly, in most cases, Surrealism is just a trick; quite a clever trick at times, but nonetheless a trick which, in this day of uncritical admiration, almost worship, of the new, the original, the bizarre, has 'caught on.' " [3] His view is supported by that of Charles E. Gauss, who sums up: "Surrealism's truth, beauty, and goodness have the qualities of utter confusion, unmotivated action, and disjunct relationships. Hence Surrealist art, stripped of much of the theoretical claptrap which it calls upon to support itself, becomes nothing more than an art of nonsense." [4] Gauss's strictures are so grave they cannot be permitted to pass unchallenged. If we are to believe him, then Surrealism is meaningless in painting and, no doubt, in poetry also. But his claim that Surrealism is unmotivated can survive only so long as it is agreed that the theory of Surrealism is, as he puts it, claptrap. On the other hand, if it may be assumed that the theoretical basis of Surrealism is—at least to the Surrealists—viable, then it must be admitted that the artistic creations of the Surrealists are justified. What gives Surrealist art its meaning, in fact, is its fidelity to the principles which have inspired it.

Such a statement evidently calls for qualification. For the attitude mirrored in literary and pictorial Surrealism is one that places the fullest responsibility upon the artist's conscience. The deliberate promulgation of techniques, often purely mechanical and sometimes childishly simple, creates a very special risk for the Surrealist. He may find himself slipping into a "manner" that reduces his art to an increasingly less meaningful exercise if he does not practice these techniques under the strictest control. He will finally find himself indulging in the form of trickery of which Hugh Philip speaks. Consequently, any satisfactory discussion of Surrealism's aims and accomplishments can take place only at the highet level of achievement, where the artist's honesty is not in doubt and the authenticity of his motives cannot be questioned. Of no form of artistic expression is it more true than of Surrealism that it can be judged solely upon the evidence submitted by its best exponents.

The search for mannerisms may lead to the conclusion that Surrealism is essentially a matter of facility. It needs therefore to be understood what terms like "highest level" and "best exponents" can mean in the context of Surrealist ambitions. Care is needed in establishing the standards by which Surrealism is to be judged.

"Is this painting or is it literature?" Alain Jouffroy has raised this question in relation to the Magritte exhibition held in Paris in the winter of 1955–56.[5] Jouffroy's conclusion is that Magritte's works come from "something other and something more than painting and literature exactly"— "They offer the mind a peculiar liberty, in which the strangest adventures are risked." So, for Jouffroy, the apparent academicism of Magritte's painting conceals "an anticonformism more profound and more sincere than that in which most abstract painters would have us believe."

As Jouffroy has noticed, academicism for Magritte is a means, and not an end. For his critics, however, it has remained an essential characteristic of his work. Here is evidenced a fundamentally different approach, frequently observable when the Surrealists and their critics speak of Surrealist art. Whereas the latter confine their attention to the means, persistently ignoring the theory supporting pictorial and literary Surrealism, the former take care to stress that their interest goes to the ends these means are intended to serve. Those critics who measure Surrealism by the yardstick of aesthetic standards in which the Surrealists have no faith, never go so far as to ask themselves, as the Surrealist must always do, what contribution is made by the painter's technique to "upset an image of the world imposed upon man." [6] Yet the Surrealists believe, as Breton wrote in his introduction to Ernst's *La Femme 100 têtes* (1929), that the particular truth of each of us is "a game of patience for which he must, from among all others and without having even seen them, seize the elements in flight." The methods utilized are simply the means by which the Surrealist artist attempts to seize the elements of which Breton speaks. In this sense, artistic Surrealism becomes an instrument designed for exploration and discovery: "a working system for acquiring knowledge," as Georges Hugnet has phrased it.[7]

If Jouffroy has raised one important question, José Pierre has drawn attention to another, when asking in the newspaper *Arts* whether a Surrealist can, in fact, be a painter.[8] As defined by Pierre, the Surrealist painter is someone who has "admitted the primacy of imagination, liberated by recourse to the subterranean forces of the mind, or the lyrical use of a sort of higher lucidity," and who then "gives himself up to verifying them by means of painting." His words permit a clearer comprehension of what Jouffroy had in mind when talking of the Surrealist painting of Magritte as resulting from "something more and something over than painting and literature." An even fuller understanding is made possible by Hugnet's remark: "There is no Surrealist art, there are only proposed means—and these proposed means are only temporary."

The Surrealists have never felt their real unity to be one of method, of technique only. They see it, on the contrary, as what Breton calls "a profound community of aim." [9] This aim is to "reach the land of desire which everything, in our time, conspires to veil and to prospect it in every direction until it delivers up the secret of how to 'change life.' " This is why Hugnet could assert that, for a Surrealist examining a picture, "only its hidden content counts." Following out here the distinction made by Breton between the manifest and latent content of art, we are better prepared to respond to the difference existing between Surrealism and other modes of artistic creation. Surrealism, Hugnet has reminded us, can never be judged by its supposed artistic quality. So the questions assuming ever increasing importance for the Surrealist are not the same as those that detain the art critic; as a brief article by André Masson makes plain.

Masson speaks of "the passionate search for the ineffable" which must be the painter's concern and which creates what he calls "a desperate breach between the content and the container." [10] And he explicitly refers to the inferiority of the means employed to the painter's highest aspirations. Here the basic misunderstanding separating Surrealist painting and its critics comes clearly to light. For the latter have remained more attentive to the container than to the content. The result is that the relative success they are willing to accord certain Surrealist pictures may not be of the kind in which the painter himself is interested. Meanwhile he, and his fellow Surrealists, may be inclined to feel satisfaction when the critic can see no grounds for congratulation. The irony of the situation is exemplified in James Thrall Soby's *After Picasso* (1935) where we find the pejorative comment: "Most Surrealists are Surrealists first and artists afterwards." What Soby suggests as a failing is, for the Surrealists, nothing of the kind. On the contrary, Man Ray speaks for orthodox Surrealism when he writes, à propos of a critic who remarked that he was a photographer before being a Surrealist: "In fact I was a Surrealist before being a photographer, and I flatter myself I have remained a Surrealist in the deepest sense of the word, as those who have defined the word have so admirably laid down its principles.[11]

The line of thought introduced by this statement is a valuable one, as it indicates that, to Man Ray, being a photographer—and a painter too—is simply part of being a Surrealist. What counts is not the artistic quality of what is created, but its Surrealist quality. The tension created by that breach between container and content of which Masson has spoken gives vitality and meaning to the Surrealist's work, and forms the underlying principle linking literary and pictorial Surrealism. Ernst, or Matta, or Lam, or Magritte all make use of painting to express an attitude, exemplified in a particular kind of pictorial material that is conditioned by the vision we have come to know as Surrealist. And the same is true for the Surrealist poets Breton, Péret and Mansour. The art of the Surrealist, in the medium of his choice, is, so long as he remains true to his calling as a Surrealist, a means of projecting, or externalizing this vision. In the task he has set himself, aesthetic considerations must of necessity give way to other concerns. And so those looking to his work for Surrealist inspiration demand the joy of discovery, the sense of release, which can come not from technical preoccupations but from a determination to make use of technique in order to penetrate to the world of the surreal.

In Surrealism, the key question ceases to be: How good a painter or a poet is the artist under discussion? It becomes instead: How well does this artist make use of his medium to project an inner vision that permits us to experience and explore the world of surreality? Thus much of what passes for critical comment about Surrealism ceases to have relevance. It seems therefore appropriate to speak less of misinterpretation than of misunderstanding. For standard critical approaches are incompatible with Surrealism as its defenders would have us understand it.

This basic incompatibility might be illustrated by innumerable examples, of which one only need be mentioned as demonstrating how easily one may be distracted from central issues. Discussing the retrospective exhibition of Ernst's work held in London in 1961, G. M. Butcher, concentrating upon the technique of *frottage,* noted: "It is not aesthetically interesting that Ernst was the inventor of these techniques, but it is of considerable importance to know that he found short-cuts around his technical limitations." [12] It may not be aesthetically interesting, but Surrealistically it is very much so. What is more, it is from the Surrealist point of view that Ernst himself has reviewed frottage, and discussed its discovery in his *Beyond Painting.* Speaking of the "insupportable visual obsession" initiated by a childhood memory of a panel of false mahogany situated in front of his bed, Ernst designates this an "optical *provocateur* of a vision of half-sleep," and in connection with it mentions his obsession with the deep grooves noticed in the well scrubbed floorboards of a seaside inn: "I decided then to investigate the symbolism of this obsession, and, in order to aid my meditative and hallucinatory faculties, I made upon the boards a series of drawings by placing on them, at random, sheets of paper which I undertook to rub with black lead." Attentive examination of these drawings resulted, Ernst assures us, in the sudden intensification of his "visionary capacities," resulting in a succession of "contradictory images superimposed, one upon the other, with the persistence and rapidity of amorous memories." [13]

At no time does Ernst speak here of the technical interest of frottage beyond that of making possible certain discoveries and revelations hitherto unknown to him. These are the advantages which hold his attention. And though one could hardly expect to find the painter discussing in this context his own technical limitations (of which, after all, he may be less aware than Butcher appears to be), one cannot but notice that the phrases he employs—"hallucinatory faculties," and "intensification of visionary faculties" especially—recur most frequently in Surrealist writing. So he comments, "The procedure of *frottages,* resting thus upon nothing more than the intensification of the irritability of the mind's faculties by appropriate technical means, excluding all conscious mental guidance (of reason, taste, morals), reducing to the extreme the active part of that one whom we have called, up to now the 'author' of the work, this procedure is revealed by the following to be the real equivalent of that which is already known by the term *automatic writing.*" [14] The real attraction of frottage is then its appearance as a valid Surrealist technique, worthy of its place besides that first discovery of automatic writing which led Breton to formulate the hypotheses upon which the *Manifesto of Surrealism* rests. And its validity is clearly related to its special characteristics and particularly to the role it imposes upon the artist who practices it. Ernst has described this role in the following terms: "It is as a spectator that the author assists, indifferent or passionate, at the birth of his work and watches the phases of its development." Thus, speaking of his own experience, Ernst could write: "In striving more and more to restrain my own active participation in the unfolding of the picture and, finally, by widening in this way the active part of the mind's hallucinatory faculties I came to assist *as a spectator* at the birth of all my works, from the tenth of August, 1925, memorable day of the discovery of *frottage*." [15]

Ernst not only confirms his role during the practice of frottage to be a passive one, but gives proof that the attraction of the method lies in its liberation of the creative act from the limitations of premeditation and preconception, with a consequent invitation to chance and suggestion to make their contribution. Thus his remarks offer several precious clues to guide us in an examination of Surrealism's attitude towards art. Only by accepting as necessary the Surrealist's disregard for traditional modes of creativity can one hope to gain a true impression of Surrealism and of the role it reserves for literature and painting. It is axiomatic in Surrealism that the act of creation is in itself of only secondary importance. What really counts is the state of mind the creative act reflects and permits to become exteriorized. The Surrealists' undeviating consistency on this point makes it all the more suprising that critics have so frequently ignored this distinctive feature of Surrealism, and have failed to accept its consequences, thus acting in direct contradiction to a whole series of pronouncements that do no more than repeat what the Surrealists said when opening their Office for Surrealist Research: "Taking into account the false interpretation of our venture stupidly widespread among the public, we make a point of declaring what follows to all blundering contemporary critics, literary, dramatic, philosophical, exegetical and even theological: we have nothing to do with literature; but we are quite capable of making use of it, as need be, like everyone else."

More is to be learned from facing the question of Surrealism's demands upon literature and painting, than from requiring that the Surrealists submit their work to critical standards satisfying enough to others, but not adapted to ensuring achievement of the aims they have in view. The Surrealists do not judge an artist simply by what he accomplishes. They consider the motives impelling him to attempt what he aims to achieve, judging their validity in the light of the principles they recognize as pertinent. E. F. Granell indicated clearly enough the approach that should be the critic's when he wrote, "I neither know how nor why one could separate 'Surrealist painting' from the 'Surrealist condition.' " [16] And José Pierre has commented pertinently of Arshile Gorky: "With Gorky as with most of the other Surrealist painters, each painting is a passionate hypothesis in response to a profound uncertainty, a fundamental doubt of the reality of life, or the grounds for social, moral, sentimental restraints. There is always the matter of answering the Kantian triple interrogation of Gauguin: 'Where do we come from? Who are we? Where are we going?' " [17]

The material of Surrealism is always a potentiality; the task of the Surrealist to bring as much as he can of that potentiality into his own experience and into that of others. In facing his task, he perceives he must choose methods that seem appropriate, whether they have been employed before or not. As the use of such means betokens a faith, they are understood to be valid for no longer than they appear to serve the cause of Surrealism. In whatever medium we choose to consider,[18] Surrealism shows itself to be motivated by one concern before all others. For the Surrealist's is, as Breton has repeatedly stressed, a human mission. Whether his images are verbal or pictorial, he never tires of the search for means to "fill in the abyss separating representation from perception," and to work for their reconciliation. The Surrealists have assumed the task of reconciling man and the universe and give their attention to discovering how this reconciliation may best be effected. Thus those for whom Surrealism is primarily a movement in painting would be well advised to reflect upon the warning underlying Breton's remark in his *Le Surréalisme et la Peinture*, that painting is a "lamentable expedient."

A SWING DOOR 4

A swing-door is in us, leading to the memory-less spaces of a metahuman condition.

Simon Hantaï & Jean Schuster

Certain generalizations regarding Surrealism recur so frequently in the critical writings it has occasioned in almost forty years that repetition has rendered them all too familiar. Of these one proposed with perhaps more confidence than all the others is the very popular supposition that Surrealism has as its essence a desire to draw upon and even imitate dream experience. The result is self-evident. If in fact Surrealism and dreaming are one and the same thing, then it is all the easier to dismiss the former as having no greater influence upon life in the real world than the latter. And the conclusion follows logically: Surrealism is conveniently classified, once its ambitions are reduced to fairly comprehensible limits that successfully render it comfortingly anodyne. If this is all Surrealism amounts to, then there is no cause for alarm.

What gives persistent vitality to this line of thought is, of course, the fact that there appears to be ample evidence to support it. The first revelation of the potential power Surrealism has sought to define and turn to account came to André Breton, by his own avowal, at a moment when he was falling asleep. It was then, as he has recorded in his *Manifesto of Surrealism* that, without warning or premeditation, a phrase seemed, he says, to *"tap at the window pane."* The famous phrase—"There is a man cut in two by the window"—intriguing in its evident gratuitousness, appeared to owe its release into the conscious mind thanks to a state of relaxation apparently closely related to Breton's drowsy condition. Having experienced its arrival, he was thus encouraged to launch the series of experiments with language from which organized Surrealism grew. These experiments, by the way, included the celebrated "period of sleeping fits," during which René Crevel, Benjamin Péret and especially Robert Desnos, having submitted to hypnotic trance, replied to questions posed by their friends. Totally indifferent, in accordance with their denial of religious faith of any kind, to any ambition to communicate with another world, the future Surrealists remained preoccupied with the novel kind of imagery liberated during hypnosis, fascinated by the curious relationship existing between sleep and the waking state. Very soon Breton was announcing in his *Manifesto*, "Freud was right to bring critical attention to bear upon the dream. It is, indeed, inadmissible that this considerable part of psychic activity . . . should have received so little attention." Breton proposed to remedy matters and from the first paragraph of his manifesto presented man as "ce rêveur définitif."

In the same year as the manifesto, appeared also Aragon's "Une Vague de Rêves," followed a year later by a whole number of *La Révolution surréaliste* devoted to dreams. Within another year Eluard's *Les Dessous d'une Vie* had been published. And evidence of interest in dreams need not be drawn solely from the very first years of active Surrealism. When *La Révolution surréaliste* was replaced by *Le Surréalisme au service de la Révolution*, space continued to be reserved for articles inspired by and examining dream experiences. The new review, it may be noted, came out in

1930, the same year as Ernst's *Rêve d'une petite Fille qui voulut entrer au Carmel,* following his *La Femme 100 Têtes* of 1929. Later still, when Breton had no longer to rely only upon dreams to give him some indication of the possibilities of Surrealism, he nevertheless accepted the task of editing a special number of the *Cahiers GLM* entirely given up to dreams, in 1938. And between whiles he had written his *Les Vases communicants* (1932), to examine the relation existing between the two "vessels" of waking and dreaming.

If a catalogue of this sort—which could readily be extended if material from later years were noted—seems to confirm the view that Surrealism is indistinguishable from the wish to identify literature and art with dream re-creation, this can only be the case if we ignore an important point that places the Surrealists' interest in dreams in correct relation to their dominant preoccupations. This is the special demand the Surrealist makes of dreams, the motivation behind the attention he gives them.

To approach this question accurately one can conveniently take as a starting point a remark by Georges Hugnet in the "Dreams" issue of the *Cahiers GLM:* "The dream tells the truth; it is revolutionary." These words call for expansion and lead to a better appreciation of the place reserved for dreams in Surrealism. But the essential has already become clear. The dream interests the Surrealist because, in Hugnet's phrase, it has the capacity to "tear up the real." In this sense dreaming becomes an instrument in Surrealism's revolt against the world of the conventional. So, though dream-transcription played its part in the preliminary exploration of possibilities which accompanied the first experiments of the Surrealists, there was no question of blind confidence. Before dreams could earn an established place in Surrealism and become the source of inspiration for one of its most vital techniques, it had to be proved they could make a direct contribution to the pursuit of the highest Surrealist ambitions. This is to say that the Surrealists' continued preoccupation with dreams is not proof of a simple desire to borrow or to imitate. It is rather the confirmation of a growing conviction that dreams may be called upon to advance proposed aims.

From the outset, of course, the dream had much to commend it, especially in view of one factor, of increasing importance as Surrealism became more sure of where it wished to go. This is the essentially passive role to which dreams reduce the dreamer. In dreams we become, to quote Pierre Mabille, "amiable spectators, and no longer intransigent masters with inquisitorial control." [1] We submit without questioning, and what we appear to see and experience offers us little surprise until we return to the waking world. Ernst's affection for frottage is evidence enough of the eagerness with which the Surrealist surrenders active control and seeks in the very processes of creation a means of creation for which he becomes less and less responsible. And the circumstances of dreaming offer this added double virtue of which Mabille speaks: its capacity to "cast light upon our true internal reality," and to "reveal new aspects of a wider external reality."

Two lines of approach are opened up by Mabille's words which introduce a point of paramount importance for the Surrealist. This has been emphasized by Breton in his *Les Vases communicants* which informs its readers that the true limit of the dream "cannot but be the life of man." Here is the focus which most clearly defines the relation of dreams to Surrealism's programme. When the Surrealists turn to dreams for inspiration, theirs is not an act of withdrawal from life. The prestige attributed to dreaming has in Surrealism nothing to do with escape. Nor is it indicative of nostalgia. Evasion is quite foreign to Surrealism, which has as its purpose to come to terms with life, not to turn away from it. Here is the delicate point of balance that has rendered the Surrealists' attitude towards dreams so fascinating and so much more complex than is generally admitted. That they should be drawn to dream experience is no surprise when one considers how dreaming guarantees incon-

gruity and a notable release from logical restraint. But if
this feeling of release may seem to denote a withdrawal from
life, the Surrealist refuses to lose sight of their determination to prove Surrealism a mode of *action*. So the Surrealist
poet, Breton promises in *Les Vase communicants*, "will sur-
mount the depressing idea of the irreparable divorce between action and dreaming." Through dreams, the Surrealist does not aspire to escape the unhappy world about him,
but to attain fuller development through self-knowledge, as
dreams tend to bring this into his experience.

"What is important to me," wrote Albert Béguin, opening
the "Dreams" number of *Cahiers GLM*, "is to know who I
am." His words echo significantly those of Breton, beginning
Nadja (1928) with the question: "Who am I?" Much of
Surrealism's interest in dreams results from the belief that
this important question will not receive a complete answer
until man has interrogated his dreams. Dreams, we are
assured in *Les Vases communicants*, help man to "accomplish the *vital leap*." Far from weakening his impulse to
react to life, to question reality, dreams become, in Breton's
phrase, "the unknown source of light destined to remind us
that at the beginning of the day as at the beginning of human life upon earth, there can be only one resource, which
is action." Just as dreams throw light upon the inner man,
so they prompt in us vital questions concerning the world in
which we find ourselves, inciting us to act upon this world, to
effect its transformation.

The Surrealist is completely disinterested in any form of
existence that it does not lie within man's power to make
his own, now, in this world. And *Les Vases communicants*,
which tells us that dreams are "not devoid of consequence
upon the plane of practical existence," adds its testimony to
an ever-increasing accumulation of documents that rein-
force the belief expressed in the first number of *La Révolution surréaliste*, by J. A. Boiffard, Roger Vitrac, and Paul
Eluard: "Now that 'knowledge' has been brought to trial
and condemned and 'intelligence' is at a discount, the dream,

the dream alone, can provide the freedom that is man's due."

Eluard has taken care, though, to dispel misunderstandings by stating uneqivocally: "There exists another world. But it is assuredly in this one." In doing so, he has highlighted one of the major tasks faced in Surrealism: that of bringing a new world out of the old. Introducing the catalogue of the International Surrealist Exhibition in London in 1936, Herbert Read explained: "The philosophers, said Marx, have only *interpreted* the world in different ways; the point, however is to *change* it. The artists, too, have only interpreted the world; the point, however, is to transform it." Sharing Gérard de Nerval's conviction that there exists a link between the inner world and the outside world, the Surrealists are persuaded that a fuller understanding of the former will advance their efforts to transform the latter.

"Across the square where crowds are dying in thousands / a man is walking a tightrope covered with moths," wrote David Gascoyne.[2] Surrealist man walks this tightrope, sustained in his urgent need to cross the square by the belief that it lies within his power to do so. Here his faith in the communication of which Breton speaks in *Les Vases communicants* assumes importance. Ever since the *Manifesto of Surrealism* the Surrealists have remained unshaken in their belief in "the future resolution of those apparently contradictory states, dream and reality, in a sort of absolute reality," that Breton chose to call *surreality*.

Within these ambitions, dreams offered the basis for the new reality which Breton's introduction to Ernst's *La Femme 100 Têtes* called "the function of our will completely to displace everything." For this reason, the Surrealist painter Victor Brauner has suggested that one of the reasons his painting should appeal to the spectator is that it is "a world of dreams."[3] But this does not mean that Brauner's painting is either comforting or escapist. There is nothing merely fanciful in his work; nothing reassuring either. So we find another Surrealist, Conroy Maddox, drawing attention to the fact that, in Brauner's pictures, everyday objects acquire "the life and function of strangely somnambulistic animals, obsessional creatures assuming an objective concrete reality." [4] Brauner's is a world that imposes itself compulsively upon us. The feeling of familiarity engendered by recognition of forms borrowed from the world around us serves only to enrich a sense of alienation that becomes increasingly difficult to communicate in rational terms. The effect is all the more disturbing for the important part reserved in Brauner for humor, a humor that does nothing to provoke in us a sense of relief.

Thus, if Mabille has been able to claim the work of Brauner to be an attempt to penetrate to an inner vision, to a world seen only with eyes closed, this is not a world of escape from the cares about us. It is, on the contrary, a world that prompts reflection about everyday reality, taken so much for granted. In this, Brauner's painting resembles that of Wolfgang Paalen, to whom the Surrealists paid this compliment: "Contrary to most painting today, which proposes solely to satisfy the pleasure of the eye, that of Paalen interrogates the visitor, and, to use the artist's phrase, asks him 'Who are you?' " [5] Both painters share fundamentally the same concerns, as we see when Brauner confesses that he paints to pass, through painting, to "the other side of everything," adding, "I don't paint to *get out*. I am already on the outside, I paint to *get in*." [6] In this, Brauner is close to Ernst's whose canvas *A l'Intérieur de la Vue* (1927) takes us "inside sight." For Brauner is the courageous dreamer painted by René Magritte in *Le Dormeur téméraire*, having the courage of his own dreams to make his painting that form of action of which the Surrealists approve. His pictures provoke disquiet and self-examination, and resist what Breton calls in *L'Amour fou*, the greatest weakness in contemporary thought: "the extravagant overestimation of the known compared with the unknown."

Breton has indicated the Surrealist viewpoint clearly enough in his *Le Surréalisme et la Peinture,* where he writes, "It is impossible for me to consider painting otherwise than as a window; my first concern is to know what it looks out upon." This basic principle of Surrealism is reaffirmed ten years later by Magritte and Louis Scutenaire, writing in *London Bulletin* in March 1929: "The real value of art is proportionate to its liberating revelation." So, as Gordon Onslow-Ford see it,[7] the most vital aspect of a canvas is "an aspect of inner vision that turns the spectator into a bridge over which the images pass from the painting into his everyday life." Those dream representations that command the Surrealist's attention are the ones that make us dissatisfied with life, and reveal to us how it may be transformed.

The belief then against which Surrealism has always violently reacted is that which assumes the artist to be capable of finding his model only in the external world. For this reason, it has found in dreams an open invitation, an affirmation, a confirmation that other worlds exist, and within our reach. Their reality depends entirely upon our willingness to bring them into our experience. Therefore the creative artist, instead of confining himself to the familiar, should reach out for the as yet unknown, to make it known to himself and to others. This does not signify that the Surrealists have been satisfied simply with the transcription of dreams, though they have fully realized how useful dreams can be in stimulating the imagination, in revealing potentialities that would otherwise remain unsuspected, in teaching man to disregard the limitations of the purely rational world. So long as dreams and waking existence are generally considered to be two separate forms of experience, the dream can be accorded little significance for life. The rational mind has so carefully insulated dream life from what is agreed to be the real that the most implausible events, the strangest spectacles encountered in dreams can very easily be dismissed when the dream is over. But the best Surrealist art would fail in its ambition if it permitted the spectator or reader such ready release from its spell. Art, however powerful its initial effect, cannot aspire to the active role Surrealism demands for it, if it can be shown to be as unrelated as dreaming is claimed to be to everyday reality. For Surrealism, despite its frequent use of humor, does not wish to amuse its public and then permit them to move on to further novelties. Genuine Surrealist art implicates its audience, and does so knowingly.

Antonin Artaud hinted as much, when he introduced the scenario of his film *La Coquille et le Clergyman* with a statement in which we read: "I will not seek to find excuse for its apparent incoherence through the facile loophole of the dream." [8] Offered as no more than the re-creation of dream experience, *La Coquille et le Clergyman* would lose much of its revolutionary force, would cease to exemplify the qualities of the Surrealist cinema as Artaud saw them: "to display the motives of our actions in their original and profound barbarity," "to administer a shock to the eye, drawn so to speak from the very substance of the eye." At the same time, when, two years later, Luis Bunuel and Salvador Dali made their film *Un Chien Andalou* (1929), a "deliberately anti-plastic, anti-artistic film," they found, by Bunuel's own confession, "a fruitful analogy" in dreams. Its plot, Bunuel has emphasized, being the result of what he calls "a CONSCIOUS *psychic automatism*," does not purport to relate a dream, but it "profits by a mechanism analogous to that of dreams." [9] The result is a film Bunuel has characterized as "freed from the ballast of reason and tradition," evidently owing this freedom to dream example, yet not produced simply by a process calculated to imitate this example. The complexity of Surrealism's attitude towards dreams is evidenced here, as it is in these words of Paalen: "The true value of the image, through which artistic activity is connected with human development, lies in its capacity to *project* a new realization which does not have to be referred for its meaning to an object already existing." The value of such an image is, Paalen affirms, not its capacity to *repre-*

sent but to *prefigure,* "to express potentially a *new order* of things." [10]

Statements like Paalen's recur with significant regularity in Surrealism and may be taken as exemplifying a persistent attitude. Writing in *Cahiers d'Art* in 1939, Joan Miró condemned as a bourgeois pastime everything that does not "disclose the activity of a mind wishing to escape from present reality, which today is particularly ignoble, and seek out new realities, offering other men a possibility of elevation." "This has always been my goal," Miró has confided to James Thrall Soby, "to transcend the purely plastic fact to reach other horizons." [11]

The origins of this attitude in Surrealism may be traced back to a date even prior to the first *Manifesto,* when Breton, writing in *Paris-Journal* on March 25 1923, made public his belief that a painting or a piece of sculpture should be considered only secondarily from the point of view of taste, and must stand or fall upon whether it "makes our abstract knowledge take a step forward." This is the attitude which leads to the affirmation in his *Manifesto of Surrealism* that "the flora and fauna of Surrealism are unavowable." Breton's views find their vindication in, for example, the painting of Ernst, who has explained in *Beyond Painting,* "Painting is not for me either decorative amusement, or the plastic interpretation of a felt reality; it must be every time: invention, discovery, revelation."

The objects and creatures Surrealism creates must impose themselves upon the imagination with all the conviction of truth—Ernst's hundred-headless woman, Breton's soluble fish and white-haired revolver, or those strange encounters recorded so faithfully in the canvases of Delvaux, Magritte, Dali, or Dorothea Tanning. The Surrealist invites his public to look before he asks them to understand. And he takes care to compel them to look, as dreams do, even when they have no expectation of understanding what they see. Thus the Surrealist—whether painter or poet—becomes, in Eluard's phrase, "a slave to the pure faculty of seeing."

Eluard, it may be noted, entitled one section of his verse collection *La Rose publique* (1934), "Poetic objectivity exists only in the succession, the sequence of all the subjective elements of which the poet is, until further orders, not the master but the slave." Taking encouragement from the fruitful results obtained by passivity in dreaming, the Surrealist becomes a *mirror* silvered with "the red flow of desire." [12] The significance of the image of the mirror in Surrealism has been explained by Pierre Mabille in the following terms: "The mirror being . . . the principal means by which the self becomes aware, it leads us, for that very reason, to become disturbed regarding the true characteristics of reality." Eluard puts it thus, in his poem "Le Miroir d'un Moment," dated 1925:

> Ce qui a été compris n'existe plus
> L'oiseau s'est confondu avec le vent
> Le ciel avec sa vérité
> L'homme avec sa réalité.[13]

When Artaud called Surrealism "an insidious extension of the invisible, the unconscious close at hand," [14] he might well have been seeking to render in a phrase the distinctive quality of the work of Yves Tanguy. Tanguy is the Surrealist painter who penetrates fearlessly into a world patently not our own and subject to laws different from those to which we are accustomed. So, as Breton has remarked, in his canvases, "to recognize or not to recognize means everything." [15] The problem is that little in Tanguy's painting is immediately recognizable. Fairly representational works like *Genèse* (1926) and *L'Extinction des Lumières inutiles* (1927) are exceptional, and notably belong to his earliest period. Even so, the curious forms presented in dramatic situations that authorize titles like *Mama, Papa est blessé* (1927) and *Quand On me fusillera* (1927) still have meaning for us. They are sufficiently allusive, or at least evocative, to inspire a feeling of recognition that may leave as soon as it appears, but will return once more. The air of uneasy familiarity Tanguy creates is all the more disturbing for an air of remoteness he gives to the scenes he paints, thanks to a gift for rendering both space and depth that his admiration for Chirico helped to develop in him. This quality of remoteness seems essential to a painter whom Breton sees as presenting "the first survey—achieved without aid of legend—of a considerable extent of the neutral world which is now in its genesis." The gradual process of extinction, inaugurated with *L'Extinction des Lumières* and culminating in *L'Extinction des Espèces* (1938) gives way to a new development between *Le Temps meublé* (1939) and *La Peur* (1949), before Tanguy's work enters its final phase, as we see it in *Mirage le Temps* (1954). His last picture, painted in 1954, a year before his death, asks urgently, *Où es Tu?*

The drama underlying Tanguy's painting is one involving forms that are at once strange and familiar, distant yet close. For this is a world in which anything can happen. As Tanguy confessed in the catalogue of an exhibition of Surrealist drawings held at the Galerie des Quatre Chemins, Paris, in 1935, "I expect nothing from my reflections but I am sure of my reflexes." "I found that if I planned a picture before-hand," he explained to Soby, "it never surprised me, and surprises are my pleasure in painting." [16] Surprise is never for Tanguy a matter of simple technical virtuosity. If he painted a canvas upside-down—or turned it upside down when he had finished it—it was to share with the spectator a sense of discovery, ensuring that his picture would not be the record of past findings, but on the contrary a means of reaching out for new ones. He found this method appropriate to the exploration of that part of his pictorial universe already revealed to him, and was consequently able to penetrate to further revelations. In this he was true to his calling as a Surrealist, true to the determination to break with the past and to exclude the preconceived idea. So his dream world brought self-fulfilment as it brought self-discovery. Inspired by this world, David Gascoyne wrote in his poem "Yves Tanguy":

> The worlds are breaking in my head
> The fuming future sleeps no more
> For their seeds are beginning to grow
> To creep and to cry midst
> Rocks of the desert to come.[17]

It is possible to follow the evolution through which the forms that inhabit Tanguy's universe pass, under our gaze. In many early canvases they are elementary, so amorphous even as to be barely allusive, and fully justifying Breton's phrase "independent markings, which melt into one another." It is only with the passage of time that Tanguy's universe takes on greater dramatic significance. Having learned from Chirico the value of deep shadow stressed with meticulous care, Tanguy now succeeds in infusing his pictures with an air of expectancy much more vital than in the languid canvases of Paul Delvaux. In such paintings as *Divisibilité indéfinie* (1942) his disquieting technique makes its fullest effect under a brilliant lighting which leaves the forms in clear definition, even though the horizon line has become disconcertingly indistinct. Now Tanguy demonstrates that he shares with Dali an appreciation of the dramatic possibilities of light. From this point on, his work becomes increasingly compelling because, though he is most careful to delineate shapes with unmistakable clarity and to place them in evident relation to other forms, we are never sure whether we are seeing them in sunlight or in moonlight. This, in fact, may be the "earthlight" that gives its name to Breton's early collection of poems, *Clair de Terre*. Certainly no source of light is ever indicated. The result is a sensation of isolation in the spectator, a feeling of distress and loneliness enhanced by the absence of any feeling of security.

Gascoyne's poem "Educative Process" evokes "Negotiations with the infinite / Upon an empty shore." Perhaps, indeed, this is what Tanguy invites his public to witness. At least we can be sure that this universe is not our own. Yet at the same time we are not entirely estranged from it. And we cannot remain indifferent to the forms presented before us. If we do not know them yet, very little—it seems—stands between us and full comprehension. As sometimes in our dreams, we are upon the brink of knowledge, for the very precise outline Tanguy gives his shapes endows them with substance, a tangible quality from which they take their credibility. Tanguy's painting represents a perpetual temptation to the spectator to reach out, to palpate forms he senses would enter more completely into his experience if he could but touch them. But how can he penetrate to them, how can be venture into a universe where no clear horizon gives confidence and stability? And were he to succeed in doing so, would not the self-sufficiency of the creatures Tanguy has drawn repel contact? These are some of the questions raised by Tanguy's inventive manipulation of perspective that is at the same time a measure of our failure to escape from this world, and of our desire to do so.

But it is not escapism that Tanguy offers. Nor is it the simple exercise of memory, drawing upon what dreams have made available. One is conscious of the painter's invitation to go further, to penetrate the mirror, to share and enjoy a freedom this world denies but which is already the prerogative of the objects he depicts. When Tanguy asks *Where are You?* he proposes no answer. We know only that this is a universe in which time has ceased to count, where space is elastic, and gravity no longer exerts its influence. So Tanguy's painting fulfils one of the prime necessities of Surrealist art. In involving the spectator, it leaves him marked by an experience as provocative as it is unfamiliar. If these pictures were without relevance for the world in which we live, they would be mere pipe-dreams. If Tanguy had painted a universe completely unrelated to the world we know, then he would be unworthy of a place among the Surrealist painters. But the dream he pursues throughout his work is that of which Karel Teige spoke in the first number of the Surrealist review *NEON:* "The dream expressed in a poem or in a picture becomes a force tending to materialize and to identify itself with life." Were it otherwise, then Tanguy's art would be no more than an amusement, a pastime. This art, however, bears comparison with the Surrealist poem, which Gaston Puel, in the third number of *NEON* called not the transcription of a dream but "its transposition into the heart of the real by the will of the quality of language to impress itself as a key to two worlds apparently dissimilar." To clarify what Puel meant, it is well to examine one such poem which will serve to summarize the Surrealists' attitude towards dreams.

The first few lines of Breton's "Vigilance," published in 1932 in *Le Revolver à Cheveux blancs* are relatively reassuring in their echoes of the verse of Apollinaire and even of Baudelaire's urban poetry:

A Paris la tour Saint-Jacques chancelante
Pareille à un tournesol
Du front vient quelquefois heurter la Seine et son ombre
    glisse imperceptiblement parmi les remorqueurs.[18]

But we soon lose the impression of being on familiar ground. From the beginning, it would seem, Breton establishes the background of Paris neither to present it in an unexpected light, as Apollinaire does, nor to seek in it the image of his own anguish, like Baudelaire, but rather to make the essential substance of his poem, the "incident" he evokes, stand out in opposition to the world we know. The movement this poem takes is away from reality, as the poet turns his back upon it. So the everyday world is a point of departure, permitting the reader to measure the distance the poet invites him to travel. In fact, reality begins to lose its stability in the very first verse, losing its capacity to restrain the poet, whose imagination is beginning to dominate it, promising him escape. "Only imagination," asserts the first *Manifesto*, "gives me an understanding of what *can be,* and this is enough to raise a little the terrible interdiction." Again in the catalogue of the International Surrealist Exhibition held in Amsterdam in 1938, we read, "In our period, only the imagination can restore to menaced man the feeling of being free."

It is the special value of "Vigilance" that it records the poet's sense of liberation and indicates that this comes to him through the imagination, in association with the freedom of the dream:

A ce moment sur la pointe des pieds dans mon sommeil
Je me dirige vers la chambre où je suis étendu [19]

Just as the hero of Artaud's film *La Coquille et le Clergyman* sees himself approach in a room in which he is standing, so the poet of "Vigilance" is released from the limitations of time and space, to remind us that Breton and Eluard wrote in their *Notes sur la Poésie:*

In the poet
It is intelligence, waking that kills;
It is sleep that dreams and sees clearly.

Therefore in "Vigilance" the poet exults in a feeling of release from himself. Entering the room in which he himself is lying, he sets fire to it:

Et j'y mets le feu
Pour que rien ne subsiste de ce consentement
qu'on m'a arraché.[20]

Just as the poet exults in a sense of release from himself, and finds in the spectacle of his own body lying in sleep a tribute to the power of dreams to bring liberation, so he symbolizes his break with the past, with all that is left behind, metaphorically dead, in the act of burning his body, typifying for him old ties. "Fire is a friend that does us a service," we read in Breton and Eluard's *L'Immaculée Conception* (1930).

In this act of sacrifice is a reminder of the Surrealists' hate for memory, castigated in Crevel's *L'Esprit contre la Raison,* and in Georges Hugnet's *Le Droit de Varech.* And so the act of setting fire to his room—imaging past associations—and of destroying his own body is a sacrificial gesture invoking the idea of transformation, echoing the last line of the *Manifesto of Surrealism:* "Existence is elsewhere." The poet's act is one of protest (reflected in the sensational image he employs) and of liberation from imposed controls. We are presented then with a process of rebirth which, through the sacrificial fire, becomes a process of initation so changing reality that:

> Les meubles font alors place à des animaux de même
>   taille qui me regardent fraternellement
> Lions dans les crinières desquels achèvent de se con-
>   sumer les chaises
> Squales dont le ventre blanc s'incorpore le dernier
>   frisson des draps
> A l'heure de l'amour et des paupières bleues.[21]

At this point the poet stresses his satisfaction at the sight of his own body consumed in flames:

> Je ma vois brûler à mon tour je vois cette cachette
>   solennelle de riens
> Que fut mon corps
> Fouillé par les becs patients des ibis du feu.[22]

For not until every trace has gone can the poet penetrate to another mode of experience, leaving the rest of humanity behind:

> Lorsque tout est fini j'entre invisible dans l'arche
> Sans prendre garde aux passants de la vie qui font
>   sonner très loin leurs pas traînants.[23]

Now the poet can gain a new sense of reality, that higher form of reality which is surreality:

Je vois les arêtes du soleil
A travers l'aubépine de la pluie
J'entends se déchirer le linge humain comme
    une grande feuille
Sous l'ongle de l'absence et de la présence qui
    sont de connivence
Tous les métiers se fanent il ne reste d'eux
    qu'une dentelle parfumée
Une coquille de dentelle qui a la forme parfaite
    d'un sein.[24]

The poet has reached a new experience in a world where
conventional rules no longer count for him. Absence and
presence are one. Time is transformed, becoming in Dali's
phrase, "the delirious Surrealist dimension *par excellence*."
No poem shows better than "Vigilance," therefore, how the
Surrealist poem, in Eluard's words, "desensitizes the Universe to the sole advantage of human faculties, permits man
to see other things in another way. His old vision is dead or
false. He discovers another world, he becomes a new man."
The first *Manifesto* phrased it more simply: "Poetry carries
within it perfect compensation for the miseries we endure."
  "Vigilance" clarifies what Breton and Eluard meant when
in their *Notes sur la Poésie* they suggested that the poem is
"a *débâcle* of the intellect," and added, "After the débâcle,
everything begins." In *Les Vases communicants*, written
like "Vigilance" in 1932, Breton wrote, "I hope that it [Sur-
realism] will be known for having attempted nothing better
than to place a conductor [*jeter un fil conducteur*] between
those all too dissociated worlds of waking and dreaming, of
external and internal reality, of reason and madness." The
image Breton chose here is the same as that which appears
in the last verse of "Vigilance":
  "Je ne touche plus que le cœur des choses je tiens le fil." [25]
In these words, the triumph of the poet over the world of
accepted reality is clearly indicated, in a phrase calling to
mind Theseus' triumph over the Labyrinth. Thanks to the
initative experience made possible by dreaming, the poet has

risen to a new plane of existence and perception, in a world which it lies within his power to explore.

The Surrealists would never claim to have been the first to draw attention to dreams as a source of inspiration and encouragement. Charles Nodier in *Sur Quelques Phénomènes du Sommeil* and Gérard de Nerval in *Aurélia*—to cite only French authors—are but two nineteenth-century writers who, in advance of Surrealism, have seen in dreams what Nerval called "a second life." But what distinguished the Surrealist's approach is the conviction, which has become a quite conscious one, that this second life has special relevance for the first life to which birth has committed us. Perpetually preoccupied with the problem of human identity, the Surrealist asks the questions formulated by Béguin in the "Dreams" number of *Cahiers GLM:* "Could I be only this self which it is so easy to circumscribe; with its narrow precise limits: in time, from my birth to my death; in extent, from my memories and my consciousness to my acts? Can I be satisfied with this self among so many, and can I suppose it to be justified?" There is no need to wonder what replies Surrealism encourages us to make, as we take these questions with us into our dreams. Thus the title of one of Roberto Matta Echaurren's pictures takes on special meaning: his *Inscape* does not represent the evasion that comes from escapism so much as the invasion of the self, a conquest accomplished in full awareness and complete sincerity. The technique the Surrealist aims to master is that of which Breton speaks in *Cahiers GLM* as suitable to achieving "a greater knowledge of the fundamental aspirations of the dreamer as well as a more precise appreciation of his immediate needs." This technique owes some of its characteristic qualities to the example of dream experience, but cannot be adequately studied solely within the confined limits of dream investigation. To grasp Surrealism in its complexity, one must be prepared to follow the Surrealists further along the path of enquiry.

OPEN SESAME 5

Beyond that savage pretence of knowledge
Beyond that posture of oblivious dream
Into the divided terrain of anguish
Where one walks with bound hands
Where one walks with knotted hair
With eyes searching the zenith
Where one walks like Sebastian.

David Gascoyne

There can be no doubt regarding the importance attached in Surrealism to automatism. The first definition of Surrealism ever proposed took in the *Manifesto of Surrealism* the form "pure psychic automatism by which it is proposed to express, either verbally, or in any other manner, the real functioning of thought." "The dictation of thought in the absence of any control exercised by reason, beyond aesthetic or moral preoccupations"—this is the interpretation Breton explicitly places upon automatism, as understood in Surrealism. Hence the history of literary Surrealism is accepted as having begun in 1919 with the texts Breton and Soupault published in *Littérature,* under the title *Les Champs magnétiques.*

From the moment when Surrealism became articulate, automatic writing has been accepted as "a magical dictation," "a veritable photography of thought." Eluard spoke for the whole Surrealist group when he announced in his preface to Gisèle Prassinos' *La Sauterelle arthritique* (1935) that automatism "forever opens new doors upon the unconscious." Not unexpectedly, therefore, one encounters evidence of extreme views regarding the importance automatism holds in Surrealism. For Hugnet, Surrealist thought is "a complete submission to the automatism of thought," the Surrealist poet a writer who "transcribes without the intervention of controlling reason." [1] While it will be necessary to treat such assertions with care, for fear of giving too much prominence to what is, after all, only one technique among several, it is unquestionable that automatism has proved to be what Hugnet calls "the open sesame" of Surrealism.

Writing in the catalogue *Surrealist Intrusion in the Enchanters' Domain* Vincent Bounoure has remarked, "Surrealism has replaced mythology with psychic automatism." Without falsifying Bounoure's thought, one might phrase it somewhat differently and say that psychic automatism is one of the great myths upon which Surrealism has built and organized its effort. With his first manifesto, Breton published the automatic text *Poisson soluble* to illustrate his contention that Surrealism has the same effect upon the human mind as narcotics, and that Surrealist images offer themselves "spontaneously, despotically" to man who cannot dismiss them once his will ceases to exert power over his faculties.[2] This belief led Breton to recommend in his *Manifesto of Surrealism* the following method for obtaining such images: "Write quickly, without a preconceived subject, quickly enough not to remember and not to be tempted to re-read." Here is the elementary technique of literary automatism in which Breton assures us we may have confidence. The fact that this method is so purely mechanical, so readily available to all inclined to practice it, makes the remarkable fidelity of the Surrealists to automatism all the more worthy of examination.

Surrealism's interest in dreams has already made clear what aims are in view: "Contrary to what spiritualism proposes: to dissociate the psychological personality of the medium," Breton explains in *Point du Jour* (1934), "Surrealism proposes nothing less than to unify this personality." In Surrealism, as a consequence, automatism is regarded as a means of revelation, especially of those levels of the human personality that dreams indicate exist beneath the surface of consciousness. "Every second," the *Manifesto* declares, "there is a phrase foreign to our conscious thought asking only to become exteriorized." Though we cannot fully comprehend this phenomenon, Breton affirms we cannot remain indifferent to its importance. So *Point du Jour* shows him to be preoccupied with "something great and obscure" that "tends imperiously to express itself through us." It is, as he has confessed, merely a matter of pursuing certain implications of methods of psychological investigation already made available to medicine.

Attached to the French Second Army psychiatric centre at St. Dizier, Breton had ample opportunity during his war service to give his attention to the methods psychiatry offered for the fuller comprehension of the human personality. At St. Dizier, he was able to experiment with patients, not only recording their dreams, but also noting their uncontrolled flow of words during free association. Indeed, the origins of the first Surrealist techniques are here. Dreams and free association are, as Breton admits in *Entretiens*, at first almost the whole of Surrealist material: "There will have been simply an amplification of *aims*," *Entretiens* explains, "thanks to which these dreams and associations are to be collected: interpretation, yes, but above all *liberation* from constraints—logical, moral and so on—with a view to recuperating the original powers of the mind."

To the Surrealist, automatism, like dreams, held the immediate attraction of release from those restraints to which Breton refers and which he deems blunting in effect upon the human mind. In contrast with the language of conventional communication, the automatic text appeared to Hugnet, for example, to be "the very activity of thought." [3] Hence its appeal as a means of illuminating the personality: "By a return to automatism," Conroy Maddox has remarked, "we see means of eliminating the boundaries and of multiplying the ways of reaching the most profound levels of the mental personality. Painting and poetry become the evocation of a spontaneous and delirious expression." [4] But the impulse which Maddox highlights is not the only one that accounts for Surrealism's persistent faith in automatic techniques. Liberty such as man knows through automatism will not simply permit him to know himself better; it will prepare him to discover more than existing conditions allow him to know. Abdication of reasoned control, surrender to the free flow of uninhibited imagination—these represent "a revolution of the mind in its reasoning and imaginative faculties, an uncompromising struggle for the absolute freedom of the individual." [5]

This wider ambition ensures that automatism does not become for the Surrealist an idle exercise of little consequence. Automatism stands as a method available to all to dredge beneath the surface of the mind and to present for examination a residuum that would otherwise escape notice. So the fact that automatic techniques are relatively easy to practice in no way affects the faith the Surrealists have retained in the importance to be attached to revelations only automatism can make possible. For this faith is firmly based upon two convictions that the passage of time has not shaken.

The first of these, as Breton has gladly acknowledged, may be traced back to Romanticism. In his *L'Art magique* (1957) he writes, "From Romanticism until now, the feeling of being moved, not to say *manipulated* by forces greater than our own does not, in art, cease to become more acute, all-embracing." At this point, Breton quotes with approbation Rimbaud's phrase: "It is wrong to say: I think. One should say I am thought." These words lead Breton to pose with particular emphasis the question: Is what we create our own? Disturbing perhaps for the creative artist concerned with a talent he feels entitled to call his own, this question in no way shakes the Surrealist's confidence in himself. For him, it is not so important to safeguard the rights of the individual temperament as to speculate upon the significance of the individual's discovery for those he invites to share his experience.

Mabille, discussing dreams in *Cahiers GLM*, already draws attention to "a sort of collective repertoire" to be noticed in a comparison of various persons' dreams. It is significant therefore that Albert Béguin has remarked in the same publication: "At the moment when I fall back upon what is most personal to me and least communicable, at the greatest possible distance from any human being, I find myself more identified with my fellow men than ever I was." Surrealism's faith in automatism denotes a profound belief in the validity of the postulation Béguin summarizes. Drawing as it does upon the collective unconscious, automatism is seen in Surrealism as a means of communication that defies and goes far beyond the limits imposed upon rational thought, by addressing its appeal to levels of the personality lying deeper than consciousness, and common to all.

The fascination of automatism for the Surrealist is that it seems to offer the possibility of creating images that are collectively comprehensible, in such a way as to realize one of his dearest ambitions; it was succinctly summarized by that forerunner of Surrealism, Lautréamont, when he wrote, "Poetry will be made by all, not by one." In the light of this aspiration, the role of the artist is modified to an important degree. He becomes, according to Eluard's dictum, not a man inspired, but a man who inspires. Thus the Surrealist view of the poet as medium commands attention once more. Through the poet certain revelations will pass into the world. So—and here is the second conviction supporting the surrealists' confidence in automatism—passivity is, for him, not a sign of weakness but a source of strength. It reflects the belief that, under certain circumstances it is the Surrealist's duty to precipitate, the poet may find himself in rapport with forces the rational mind cannot even perceive. At such times, it is his function to record, to become a channel through which inspiration can make its influence felt in the experience of his public. The claim that passivity is a valid technique in the revolt against the conventional world attests the Surrealists' faith in certain forms of association of which automatism is not the least impressive. The whole orientation of Surrealist thought on this matter is condensed in J. F. Chabrun's affirmation: "We do not believe, if truth be told, that thought sets out to conquer the image, but on the contrary that the image sets out to conquer thought." [6]

If this supposition is valid, then the adoption of complete passivity is essential in those wishing to capture as many images as they can. So the consequences of the Surrealist attitude are far-reaching. They not only pose the question of the artist's relation to his public—already raised by Dada—but bring under discussion the very nature of creative experience. The Surrealist gladly abdicates his creative personality, as this has been traditionally understood. But in return he believes himself placed in possession of what Breton calls, in *La Position politique du Surréalisme,* "the key to a treasure trove." But, as Breton states with some care, "this latter does not belong to him; it becomes impossible for him, even by surprise, to attribute it to himself: *this treasure trove is a collective one.*" Here is stressed the function of automatism, designated in Breton's *Entretiens* as being the creation of a *climate:* "the mind has got wind of a country in which flora and fauna are most recognizable but above all whose structure, apparently the same for all, asks only to be revealed."

Regarded as one of the "new keys" Surrealism places in man's hands, automatism offers access to the true life, which Rimbaud had said is absent. But a serious difficulty remains:

How to lead man to undertake the task of exploring the country Surrealism brings within range? More especially, how to make them understand, as *Entretiens* puts it, that the country is not *elsewhere* but *in themselves?* They must be persuaded of the necessity to leave behind their heavy baggage, so as to be able to "cross with lighter step the bridge leading to it." We find indicated here the elements of a programme in relation to which Paalen called the methods of automatism "various kinds of techniques of *divination*" the function of which is to sense unexpected images in "aesthetically amorphous material." [7] Though meant to apply to pictorial automatism, Paalen's words serve equally well to spotlight the question of the relationship the Surrealists would have automatism bear to poetry. In this connection, a valuable statement in Eluard's *Donner à Voir* (1939) warrants citation, as it establishes that Surrealism sees nothing inconsistent in the poet's role when he appeals to automatism. "People have thought that automatic writing has rendered poetry useless. No: it augments, simply develops the field of examination for poetic consciousness, enriching it. If the consciousness is perfect, the elements which automatic writing extracts from the inner world and the external world balance one another." It is by this process that the Surrealist poet becomes, to use Eluard's phrase, "a contagious phenomenon."

Elsewhere the Surrealist poet is defined as "a spring, producing naturally pure water." [8] Thus Breton and Eluard in *Notes sur la Poésie* (1936) assert that "by the least erasure the principle of total inspiration is ruined." For, Eluard notes in *Donner à Voir*, "Imagination has no instinct for imitation. It is the spring and torrent in which one cannot move upstream." The universe of Surrealist imagination is, consequently, a universe without a god, since it does not lie, since it never confuses "that which will be with that which has been."

Concerned with "that which will be"—"Surrealism," remarks Breton, "is what WILL BE"—the Surrealists have come to place the greatest faith in automatic principles. But they have not evaded the responsibility of considering the consequences of an attitude requiring that the products of automatism remain inviolate, with no concessions being made to the tastes, thought, or emotions of the public. Discussing in a newspaper interview the reproach of obscurity which their intransigence has earned the Surrealists, Breton has commented that it results from the over-estimation of *one* of the virtues of language: "its power of immediate exchange." [9] But care must be taken in the evaluation of Breton's statement that the Surrealist offering texts "taken down at the dictation of the inner voice," declines any responsibility for their "non-clarity." The responsibility the Surrealist will not accept is a responsibility to his public's rational sense of logic and sequence. Therefore Breton's next words assume prominence: "You know, indeed, that in Surrealism, the stress has been removed from the *I*, always more or less despotic, to the *self*, common to all men." Here is the Surrealist's authority for ignoring preconceptions and conventions. Breton's remark bears witness to a change of focus entitling Zdenko Reich to affirm: "Poetry realizes at one and the same time the unity of the dream and of human desire for knowledge." [10] So the essential feature of Surrealism, as defined by Breton, is to have proclaimed "the total equality of all normal human beings before the subliminal message," and to have maintained that this message constitutes a common patrimony. [11]

Developing and adapting certain of the attitudes of Dada toward language, Surrealism resists the stasis of the poem in favor of the generative activity of poetic creation. Meanwhile the belief in the revelatory power of the *logos* leads to the identification of uncontrolled thought with vital poetic achievement. So the Surrealists have wished to withdraw words from their utilitarian use, in an attempt to emancipate them and return to them full power. It was only to be expected that, with such ends in mind, Surrealism should have placed automatism high on the list of revolutionary techniques.

A full appreciation of the value attributed to automatism in Surrealism cannot be achieved without some consideration of the specific quality distinguishing the Surrealist image. The image claimed Breton's attention in his first *Manifesto,* where the following fundamental profession of faith finds expression: "It is so to speak from the fortuitous juxtaposition of two terms that comes a peculiar light, *the light of the image,* to which we shall reveal ourselves always sensitive. The value of the image depends upon the beauty of the spark obtained; it is, consequently, a function of the difference in potential between the two conductors." If there is hardly any vitalizing spark in the comparison as it is usually found, much greater illumination must be obtainable by confronting two very distant realities. Therefore Breton in the name of Surrealism denies that the second term may be deduced from the first *with a view to producing* the desired spark. To be worthy of the Surrealist's attention, both terms must be produced, he says, simultaneously. In the method Breton recommends, the role of reason is reduced to recognizing the luminous effect produced by means owing nothing to its intervention. Having reminded his readers that a longer spark may be produced if the electrical experiment is carried out in rarefied gas, Breton remarks, by analogy, "the Surrealist atmosphere created by mechanical writing, which I have made a point of placing at the disposal of all, lends itself particularly well to the production of the most beautiful images." It is then automatism which leads from one term of the image to the other. Eluard has reaffirmed this when writing that the mind does not lead the image but is, so to speak, led by it, so that it "gradually becomes convinced of the supreme reality of these images." The role accorded to automatism in the kind of exploration and discovery that is central to Surrealism is here made quite clear. Automatism is liberation, which is revolution, which is, in turn, both revelation and discovery. This is why "Surrealist images are never well-behaved, they scratch and bite, strike out, clear a way to new reality, to reality at last adjusted to the high level of regal desire." [12] The Surrealists' identification of automatic processes with the fulfilment of desire could not be made plainer.

If, though, the importance of automatic techniques in precipitating the kind of verbal image in which the Surrealist is interested may be recognized without difficulty, this by no means proves that automatism has anything to offer the painter in his efforts to break with convention and arrive at a new vision. How may the painter in his turn hope to present valid equivalents for the sort of imagery we find so frequently in Benjamin Péret? There is evidence that this question has not been answered to the Surrealist's satisfaction without some careful reflection. Breton has confessed [13] that he and his friends were still debating in 1925 whether or not the art of painting could be brought within Surrealist imperatives, these being understood at that time to be particularly related to automatic methods. It was in fact some time before Breton himself felt confident enought to detect genuine Surrealist elements in—to take an example—the collages produced by Ernst as early as 1920. In Ernst's frottages, dating from 1925—in which, we have had occasion to see, Ernst himself has recognized a significant degree of automatism, ensured by the purely mechanical process from which they resulted—we do find evidence of a graphic automatism which may be accepted as the equivalent of automatic writing. But there is no denying that Surrealism, having begun as essentially a literary phenomenon, passed through a period of hesitation before painting was accepted as a valid means of revealing and prospecting the surreal.

At first indeed, Pierre Naville expressed serious doubts regarding the possibility of adapting painting to Surrealism. It was to combat these views that Breton undertook a series of articles, to be published in 1928 under the still rather cautious title *Le Surréalisme et la Peinture*. Squarely facing the central problem of identifying a pictorial equivalent for automatic writing, Breton asserted that automatism in painting could supply *"rhythmic unity,"* which he felt it to be the painter's duty to supply, through the substitution for exterior reality of what he called "psychic reality, subject to the pleasure principle alone."

Looking for some practical exemplification of Breton's theories, we may find them in the method of André Masson, who has spoken as follows during his *Entretiens avec Georges Charbonnier* of his technique at the time when his work began to attract Breton's attention: "At that time I was doing pictures that without being very characteristically Surrealist, represented for all that a sort of liberty. I started with broad layers of color, and it was from the moment when these layers became insufficient for me that I added lines, and little by little arrived at the theme." What is significant here is the painter's willingness to let the theme of his picture suggest itself to him, without following any preconceived purpose, or seeking to reproduce any pre-established model. Masson evidently found inspiration not in the outside world, but in the pleasure principle to which Breton attached so much importance. The absence of a subject devised in advance is further evidenced in Masson's habit of postponing the choice of a title until his canvas was complete. "At the very outset of his search," Breton comments, "Masson came upon *Automatism,* which almost literally gave wings to the painter's hand. Not content to trace the mere shape of objects, this hand, enamoured of its own movement and of that alone, described spontaneous figures within which, as experience was to show, these shapes were destined to be embodied." [14] "Often I feel I have no need of images. I have only to let my brush run," remarked Masson, "But when the image appears, I do not chase it away, I accept it, I even multiply it." [15] Masson's words give substance to Breton's claims that would otherwise appear rather extravagant. Confidence in the advantages of passivity and in the benefits of automatism leads the Surrealist to the conviction that the images he puts on paper or on canvas are *destined* to find expression, to be communicated through the medium of his sensibility. At no time are the beneficent revelations of automatism in doubt, for they are seen as closely related to man's desire. In the "Prologue" to his *Anatomy of My Universe* (New York in 1943), Masson asserts:

This graphic world is a universe that I create. It is composed of images that fill my expectation, signified by the sheet of white paper. Whence come these imagined forms? They come from my impassioned meditation, an attitude that poses an object, even in its first movement when it seems to be completely sunk in the undetermined. But soon, as in the process of dream-inducing hallucination, or after a first stage composed uniquely of vertical schemas, there appear forms already plastic like dreams and this meditative disposition calls up forgotten sensations, buried dreams. It is their polymorphous play that I orchestrate in their becoming.

It is noticeable that, as described here, Masson's method takes advantage of passivity to furnish him with a key to a new experience, or at least provides him with the means to bring to the surface of consciousness an experience he does not fully recognize until it has already been transmitted to paper or canvas. Trust in the power of techniques such as this releases the Surrealist painter from the limitations imposed by everyday reality, introducing him to that higher form of reality which is Surrealism's concern, a surreality becoming gradually familiar to him and to his public. Masson's comments in his "Prologue" are consequently of some significance:

I let my reason go as far as it can. It traverses the court of objects and reaches finally a waste-land of infinite desolation; it is a *truly human* place, which creates its own Time.

Here, a prisoner escaped from Plato's cave, I shall no longer be subject to his condemnation of imitated reality. I would be only a point of intersection, a magnetic needle, a medium. Yet in this desert of being, where nothing can distract me, I shall realize whatever I imagine—whatever I dispose of Possibility.

There is no need to stress at this point that Masson's words prove how successfully Surrealism has assimilated pictorial automatism which becomes, as much as any other technique the Surrealists have favored, a form of action. Gordon Onslow-Ford has testified that it was automatism, as Surrealism taught him to practice it, that gave him his first visions of "the transparent, interpenetrating worlds of the mind." [16] And Conroy Maddox has added his testimony: "The creation of the *poetic image* takes us into the very heart of unconscious processes, and it would seem that any exploration aimed at its rationalization must proceed from a natural disquietude." [17] The attempt to impose rationally acceptable boundaries upon these unconscious processes must inevitably fail, as their virtue, to the Surrealist, is in their denial of such boundaries. The standards Surrealism sets up and uses to judge artistic effort transpose everything to quite a different plane. So we find José Pierre commenting as follows upon the painting of Oyvind Fahlström: "There one undertakes and sometimes not without difficulty, a descent into the maelstrom of which one cannot say whether it is a voyage to the centre of the flesh or a dive into the labyrinth of the subconscious, or a spelaelogical incursion into the mother-earth of ancestral myth." [18] For the equivocal quality of much Surrealist painting is frequently a necessary consequence of the part played in its initiation by automatic practices. Consideration of a variety of Surrealist canvases suggests the conclusion that in many of them the artist has simply painted his way out of a situation, psychological, emotional, or even ethical, by a process more intuitive than reflective. Here, for instance, are the comments with which Arp, in *On My Way* (1948), accompanies the reproduction of a picture entitled *Végétation:*

The black grows deeper and deeper, darker and darker before me. It menaces me like a black gullet. I can bear it no longer. It is monstrous. It is unfathomable.

As the thought comes to me to exorcise and transform this black with a white drawing, it has already become a surface. Now I have lost all fear, and begin to draw on the black surface. I draw and dance at once, twisting and winding, a winding, twining, soft white flowery round. A round of snakes in a wreath. . . . white shoots dart this way and that. Three of them begin to form snakes' heads. Cautiously the two lower ones approach one another.

For the true Surrealist, each picture, like each poem, is a wager, or a journey into the unknown. To begin with, the artist can never be quite sure where he will be led, or even that his journey will reach a satisfactory conclusion. In the circumstances, success and failure may often be separated only by a hair's breadth. This is why so many of the products of Surrealism find their value more in what they attempt than in what they achieve. So the Surrealist's use of automatic techniques is linked with a seriousness and sense of responsibility that one might expect to find excluded by their very use. Miró's definition of his method as one of "timing images and sensations with the greatest exactitude possible, with no mental reservations," [19] serves consequently just as well to describe the working method of the poet employing automatic techniques as that of the painter.

"I have built you wildly / And without afterthought," wrote E. L. T. Mesens in his poem "Le Mari aride." Surrealism produces without forethought either, the Surrealist being content to watch the controls exercised by conscious thought drop away, as he abandons himself to automatism, which represents for him more than a slap in the face of convention, and is not simply the excuse for uninhibited self-expression. If, through techniques inspired by dreams, the Surrealist aspires to become a mirror, automatism is for him "already being on the other side" of the mirror.[20] He looks to automatism to take him further, to place him, and—thanks to the contagious quality his work will have— his public too, already in that domain which dreams can only reflect and incite him to penetrate.

In view of the importance Surrealism attaches to automatic practices, it is only to be expected that these are not submitted to any interference from aesthetic considerations. What remains important is the act of transmission, which makes automatism a method of obtaining knowledge. Its efficacy is linked in the mind of the Surrealist too closely with its immediacy for its discoveries to be assessed coldly, especially in the light of reason. Not that this should be interpreted as meaning that the material released by automatism must appear invariably acceptable to the Surrealists. It would be ingenuous to suppose that everything owing its origin to automatic techniques must be regarded, for that sole reason, as viable. And it would be foolish to disregard how conveniently this mechanical method of creation may be offered as an excuse and even authority for something that remains not only devoid of meaning but without pertinence. In spite of its evident appeal as a method which may be promoted as consistent with Surrealism's wish to place at the disposal of mankind a practical means of escaping the confines of the everyday world, one of the most notable exponents of automatism has remarked, "I have always compared it to fishing: You may bring home a trout or an old shoe. . . . You see! Automatism is an expedient." [21]

But all Surrealist techniques are mere expedients, their value, like that of the media which favor their adoption, strictly proportional to their revelatory power. That automatism has been successfully promulgated as a worthwhile artistic method, practiced with assiduous care, and judged by the Surrealists as having fulfilled their expectations—this is enough. For automatism marks a further step away from conventional reality toward surreality, in the direction indicated by dream experience. The results it has made possible serve to show why the Surrealists have attempted to take matters further in confirming a growing faith in the efficacy of anti-rational processes of creative activity. The rewards of automatism are not without significance in prompting the Surrealists to place their confidence more and more in irrational means.

The step in this direction marked by automatic practices is an important one for Surrealism. For automatism, while it releases the Surrealist from the restrictive claims of the reality about him, also undermines the obligation to which habit may have committed him: to discuss and represent human desires rationally. In doing so, it takes literature and art even further out of the control of accepted language, both verbal and pictorial. Automatism has done Surrealism the signal service of setting the mind free to roam a world that present-day existence keeps from us. Even more important, it places in the hands of the Surrealists a method of reporting back discoveries, ensuring the maintenance of communication with those who have not as yet progressed so far. In this way Surrealism's use of automatism represents an affirmation of two basic principles. The first of these, prepared by Dada, is total indifference on the Surrealist's part to the preservation of the private artistic personality. Thus if a Surrealist painter or poet deserves admiration and thanks, it is not for the elaboration of a private language or the projection of a particular "manner," but because his language is a communicable one, capable of supplying us with the means to grasp and examine reality transformed by his hands, its elements arranged in a new revelatory order. Automatism stands, in this sense, for a protest against human vanity, and the inevitable immobility to which the artist is committed by adherence to a "style." Automatism, on the contrary, denotes the release of the subconscious in the face of social restraint. Its essential value to the Surrealist is its eruptive quality that permits it to be considered one of those "probes," which, Breton has informed us, Surrealism has sought to make available. And, thanks to the stern dictates that give Surrealism its dominant unity, the value of automatism is directly proportionate to its success in fulfilling the role for which it is intended.

So here is the second fundamental trend of Surrealism, as it is evidenced in the practice of automatic techniques. Despite their widespread reputation for obscurity, the Surrealists have never wavered in their belief that the new keys they wish to offer must be available to all who desire to use them. The Surrealists may have preferred to discourage free contact with the general public, and during the early years of their activity especially may have followed perhaps too readily Dada's lead in antagonizing a society believed to have fallen into stagnation. Much of the violence of Aragon's Surrealist writing, for instance, seems to have been a legacy of his association with Dada, in the days when

abuse was not only pleasure but an excellent means of adver-
tisement as well. Although always eager to accept the opportunity to expound Surrealist principles in any manner
presenting itself—through lectures, tracts, collective exhibitions, catalogues, reviews and even radio interviews—the
Surrealists have shunned direct intercourse, as though
popularization might prove to be some sort of compromise.
The resulting feeling of exclusion generally felt by the public
seems supported by the hermeticism that is characteristic of
a notable proportion of Surrealist art and literature. The
public face of Surrealism is, indeed, so misleading that many
have been left with a sense of frustration that has delayed
unduly the impact of Surrealism on all except a restricted
audience. And the whole matter has been further complicated by the fact that, in approaching Surrealism, too many
have adopted a point of view—or at least a point of departure—diametrically opposed to that of the Surrealists themselves, and have then complained that they do not understand. Yet the practice of automatism alone should suffice to
make clear one of the essential convictions the Surrealists
share: thoughts and feelings do not have to be rationally
comprehensible to be communicated; one does not have to
understand Surrealism to participate in its search or in its
revelations. There is a logic here that has too often passed
unnoticed. Surrealism ceases to be generative at the moment
when it becomes explicative. One may go further, and suggest that true Surrealism defies explication, but is no less
compelling for that. The response it demands owes nothing
to the intervention of the rational mind. The Surrealist
image therefore—be it pictorial or verbal—having found
release through automatism, makes its appeal not to the
mind, or to the aesthetic sense—free to accept or reject, to
balance and compare—but to deeper levels of the human
personality, where rejection is instinctive, and acceptance
intuitive.

It will remain one of the distinctions of Surrealism that
its defenders have perceived that "the bars are on the inside

of the cage," [22] and that they have sought to remove them, to liberate man from the prison of the self, to encourage him to take advantage of anything promising continued and enlarged liberty, however fortuitously the discovery may come.

ORACULAR REPLIES 6

*When Surrealism interrogates chance, it is
to obtain oracular replies.* Georges Hugnet

The practice of automatism in Surrealism complements another widespread technique, aimed at invoking as directly as
possible the contribution of chance during artistic creation.
For this reason the totally unpredictable nature of automatism's revelations can never seem to the Surrealist either
a cause for alarm or a reason to question the efficacy of his
method as a means of attaining the surreal. Here, on the
contrary, lies the very fascination of automatism: much of
its meaning comes from the fact that it takes fullest advantage of chance discovery. And here lies a notable departure from Dadaist usage. In Dada, appeal to chance stood
usually for nothing more than the rejection of traditional
creative modes. However, while iconoclasm is not without its
attraction for the Surrealists, their preoccupations have led
them to demand much more of chance than merely the form
of release the Dadaists found in it. Just as they believe it
beneficial to abdicate self-control and the projection of a
private individuality through the use of automatism, so the
Surrealists have turned to chance with certain hopes in the
forefront of their minds. They are satisfied that, by placing

their art at its disposal, they will gain immeasurably in understanding of a higher law which Arp has spoken, in *On My Way*, as sometimes sensed in our day-to-day existence. Chance alone, the Surrealist believes, will bring human activity into harmony with it.

More of the lore of Surrealism takes on a comprehensible pattern when viewed in relation to the belief Arp has made explicit. Unexpected meetings, curious coincidences, moments of prophetic insight, as we see these repeatedly attract and hold the attention of the Surrealists, all these bear witness to the conviction that the key to human existence may be found, once man has learned how to search for it. That feeling of paradise lost, underlying many of the pessimistically inclined statements dating from the early days of Surrealism, has prompted the Surrealists to be especially responsive to any means presenting the possibility of reentry to a life the world about us denies us. Breton has related in *Les Pas perdus* how, at one period in his life, he would leave open the door of his hotel room, "in the hope of finally awakening by the side of a woman companion whom [he] had not chosen." Out of context, this remark would appear naïve, or even frivolous. But, considered with similar confessions of readiness, on the part of other Surrealists, to place themselves at the disposal of whatever power may offer the opportunity to witness the reorientation of their own lives, Breton's gesture takes on a ritual character. It points to the redemptive value Surrealism attributes to an experience—the actual nature of which is less significant than its effects—initiated by chance, and at man's express invitation. Breton's behavior clearly points up the Surrealists' persistent desire for something more, something other, something which everyday life does not offer. It betokens that state of receptivity from which Surrealism originated, and which has ensured vital awareness in the Surrealists ever since.

Like the mysterious creature of whom he writes, in *Les Pas perdus,* that she was but glimpsed, one day, by a friend and himself, the central figure of *Nadja* is, by Breton's own admission, representative in his mind of "a signal of invisible complicity." The revelation of this complicity occurred, as *Nadja* relates, thanks to a chance encounter, and owed its effect on Breton's imagination to this very fact, coming as it did to support a faith in the beneficent intervention of chance in human destiny. Such incidents as the one recounted at length in *Nadja* demonstrate conclusively to what degree Surrealism remains a state of mind, admirably reflected, incidentally, in Philippe Soupault's apparently meaningless act of calling at several unlikely houses to ask if Philippe Soupault was at home. Breton, who recorded this fact in a footnote to his *Manifesto of Surrealism*, stressed its true significance from the Surrealist point of view when he remarked of Soupault, "He would not have been surprised, I think, at an affirmative reply. He would have gone and knocked on his door." Soupault's expectation of the seemingly impossible attests a reliance on chance which animates Aragon's *Le Paysan de Paris,* where one reads: "During those magnificent, sordid times, I lived by chance, in the pursuit of chance, which alone of all the divinities had succeeded in retaining its prestige."

Chance has continued to be, for the Surrealists, a divinity to be invoked, adored, interrogated. It assumes the qualities of a kind of divine grace which, they hope, will lead man back to the paradise he has lost. What then if man does place himself in rapport with chance and yield to its dictates? This is a question the Surrealists have not neglected to pose and attempt to answer from practical experience. Breton has related how, during the war, he and Jacques Vaché would go together to one of the local cinemas in Nantes, taking care not to note the times of performances so as to arrive at no prearranged hour. They would leave the cinema of their arbitrary choice at the first sign of boredom and, without taking the trouble to ascertain the title of the film they had just sampled, enter another where they behaved in the same way. The result was a succession of unrelated visual impressions, juxtaposed entirely according to chance. But their effect, Breton tells us, was "magnetizing." "What was important was that we came out 'charged' for a few days." [1]

But there is something more to note in the Surrealists' attitude toward chance and to the discoveries it makes possible. These discoveries are deemed not simply to ensure for man a sense of release from irksome restrictions. They are seen also as representing a direct response to human desire. This feature of Surrealist thought found dramatic expression in December 1935 when the review *Minotaure* published the findings of an enquiry, devised by Breton and Eluard in the following terms: "Can you say which has been the capital encounter of your life? To what degree did this meeting seem to you—does it seem to you—to be fortuitous? to be necessary?" The very orientation of these questions indicates the wish to uncover a sense of inevitability in the revelations of chance, viewed in relation to desire, that motive force of action recognized in Surrealism as dominant.

Here is the origin of the Surrealists' continued interest in chance, and of what their review, *La Brèche,* has called in its initial number, their "tireless search for the phenomena of objective hazard." Identification of such phenomena represents, in Surrealism, "an auscultation of the imaginary." This is the reason why the Surrealist will never fail to respond to those "perpetual solicitations," which Breton says in *Nadja* come from *"outside."* Always present in Surrealist thought is the conviction that the secret of their fortuitous arrangement can be found only if we are ready to interrogate ourselves as much as the world about us. Chance, in Surrealism, is a double key—to man and to his world.

It is from this viewpoint that certain Surrealist objects may best be considered. These are objects of which Breton speaks in *Nadja* as indicating "a new scale of things." Among them, and especially deserving of attention at this stage, are those which chance itself has brought to the Surrealists' attention: the *objets trouvés.*

In his *L'Amour fou*, Breton devotes considerable space to discussion of "found objects," those materializations of benevolent chance, which offer the Surrealist encouragement along the road to the surreal. Some of these, in fact, may be accepted without modification—or as the Surrealist puts it "correction"—as their form is significant enough as it presents itself to offer full satisfaction. Among these are the mask and spoon found by Breton and Giacometti in the Paris flea market. These have been fully described (and their photographs reproduced) in *L'Amour fou*, where Breton claims their discovery to have been made in response to a *necessity*. For him, the spoon seemed to respond to a need which had declared itself in a recent dream. In Giacometi's case, the mask helped to complete a carving at a time when he was having difficulty in modelling appropriate features for it. The identification of chance with the fulfilment of desire could not be clearer, and we find Breton concluding that the *objet trouvé* rigorously performs the same function as the dream, in "liberating the individual from paralysing affective scruples, comforting him and leading him to understand that obstacles he might consider insurmountable have been cleared."

The point Breton so forcefully makes in *L'Amour fou* is an important one for an understanding of Surrealism's attitude toward chance. This is a matter of such significance that Breton returned to it in an article written for the first issue of *La Brêche* in 1961 :

By the quite intermittent experience I have had of it, I am disposed to admit that the phenomena called by me phenomena of "objective hazard" (to confine myself to the terminology of Hegel) come into play only precisely when it is the heart, not the mind, which is alerted. If I have felt entitled to say this chance reveals itself as "the form of manifestation of exterior necessity making its way into the human consciousness," I make a point of adding today that such an operation has hope of starting, and, with greater reason, of reaching fruition, only to the extent that it is the heart that supplies the fuel.

The correlation of chance and human desire is here unequivocally emphasized, as it is in such remarks as these, which we owe to Breton's followers: "Desire always *discovers* the object which permits it to take form." [2] "And we see in another world the dark image of our desire." [3] In Surrealism, then, desire allies itself with chance to increase man's power over the world of accepted, unresponsive reality.

Here is a central characteristic of Surrealist thought, as we find it reflected in an article on the Surrealist object, published by Conroy Maddox in the last number of *London Bulletin* (1940) : "These objects reflect a universe brought back to life. Obeying only the laws of chance or psychic necessity, they establish a kind of canon of the unexpected, lending coherence to a dream world which identifies itself with a new and exciting poetic experience." "Every piece of flotsam that comes to hand," Breton sums up in the catalogue of the celebrated exhibition of Surrealist objects in 1936, "must be considered a precipitate of our desire."

Needless to say, man must respond to objects chance brings to his notice. Their validity can be measured only in proportion to the degree of response they evoke in him. For, to the Surrealist, chance, being creative, has an inspirational role; being revelatory, it is revolutionary, finding expression in objects which force themselves upon man's attention. As Crevel puts it in his *Le Clavecin de Diderot* (1932), Surrealist objects are "objects for thinking amorously: poetry thus erects bridges in one way and another, from the object to the image, from the image to the idea, from the idea to the precise fact. It is the route between the elements of a world which the necessity to take into account time has isolated, the route that leads to those staggering meetings to which the paintings and collages of Dali, Ernst and Tanguy bear witness."

As Crevel intimates, if not strictly *objets trouvés*, the Surrealist collages owe their existence to chance, thanks to the assistance of automatism. In the famous article "Inspiration to Order," reproduced in his *Beyond Painting,*

Ernst has defined the collage as "the exploitation of *the fortuitous encounter upon a non-suitable plane of two mutually distant realities.*" The collages of Ernst and E. L. T. Mesens give validity to Ernst's claim that, by the use of this technique, Surrealism has been "led from surprise to surprise." Taking as his example the celebrated Lautréamont image—"beautiful as the chance meeting upon a dissecting table of a sewing-machine and an umbrella"—Ernst explains why this should be so:

Let a ready-made reality with a naive purpose apparently settled once for all (i.e. an umbrella) be suddenly juxtaposed to another very distant and no less ridiculous reality (i.e. a sewing-machine) in a place where both must be felt as *out of place* (i.e. upon a dissecting table), and precisely thereby it will be robbed of its naive purpose and its identity; through a relativity it will pass from its false to a novel absoluteness, at once true and poetic: the umbrella and the sewing-machine will make love. This very simple example seems to me to reveal the mechanism of the process. Complete transmutation followed by a pure act such as the act of love must necessarily occur every time the given facts make conditions favourable: *the pairing of two realities which apparently cannot be paired on a plane apparently unsuited to them.*

Collages are endowed with deep meaning for the Surrealist because they offer directly an insight into a world where, as Breton wrote, "the distinction between the necessary and the accidental has been lost." Unfettered by utilitarian claims, objects and elements are transfigured. The effect is analogous to that encountered in genuine Surrealist poetic images, so that we find Breton prefacing an Ernst exhibition with the words: "The marvellous faculty of reaching two distinct realities, without leaving the field of our experience, and, at their coming together, of drawing out a spark, of putting within reach of our senses some abstract figures carrying the same intensity, the same relief as the others; and in depriving ourselves of a system of reference, of displacing ourselves in our own memory—that is what, provisionally, holds us."

The words with which Breton's statement concludes embody a significant postulation: "Who knows if, thus, we are not preparing ourselves to escape some day the principle of identity." Through consideration of Ernst's collages, Breton finds himself returned to one of the classic problems of Surrealism: the problem of human identity. Transposing the words with which *Nadja* closes—"Beauty will be CONVULSIVE or will not exist"—Ernst significantly concludes in *Beyond Painting:* "IDENTITY WILL BE CONVULSIVE OR WILL NOT EXIST." What it is important to notice is that in seeking to throw light upon this problem, the Surrealists have turned to chance, and in doing so have stressed the supreme necessity for passivity upon the part of the artist. As is the case in the practice of automatism, passivity is here regarded as the only suitable state of receptivity. The artist is enjoined to take what is offered him, finding through passivity rewards that might otherwise elude him.

But Ernst emphasizes that if the final product is what it must be to satisfy the Surrealist—the exteriorization of that which is "visible within us"—then the revelations of chance, like those of automatism in certain of its forms, may have to be completed by some contribution that can come only from the artist himself, and that will have for effect the fuller development of the discovery initiated by his technique. This inter-action of passive receptivity and deliberate exploitation might appear to be an impossible ideal, or even a very dangerous one, were it not that the Surrealist remains convinced he has no cause for alarm or for doubt: both automatism and the use of techniques to induce chance revelation are deemed by him to be means for uncovering in man desires that might well remain secret even from man himself. The techniques he uses prompt him to admit these desires, to render them explicit and, in the process, to learn more about himself.

Thus the new emphasis stressed in Ernst's chapter "Inspiration to Order" is by no means illogical and fully justifies the title chosen for this essay. Concerned, in utmost fidelity to Surrealist principles, with devising and developing methods to permit more ready penetration to the world of the surreal, and a more thorough exploration of its possibilities, intent, furthermore, upon establishing methods that will release him from the limitations implicit in traditional approaches, Ernst has discovered that certain mechanical means—not far removed from those of pure automatism which he, among others, has explored—can serve the artist as a starting-point, and place him *beyond* painting in the accepted sense. These he explicitly calls "means of forcing inspiration." This act of forcing is for him, and for those who have followed his example, a deliberate attempt to discover the initial impetus necessary for attempting "the vital leap." So, though the movement followed during the act of creation may appear to mark a return to a personally expressive art—an attempt to impress upon the finished product the stamp of individuality, once the benefits of chance have been turned to account—what is important in the final analysis is the degree to which this product testifies to a discovery, marks a revelation to which the artist will have made his contribution, but that impresses most as the projection of fundamental desires in which all men share.

The Surrealist, as a consequence, will enter into enthusiastic and optimistic collaboration with chance. So both his humility and pride are evidenced in titles like Ernst's *Vision Induced by a Piece of String I Found on my Table.* The artist does not deny that his vision was induced by circumstances outside his control; but he is proud that this vision has been granted him and that he has become the medium for its communication to the world. So the readiness with which the Surrealist accepts chance revelations and suggestions is a token of his assurance that chance may serve to guide him out of this world and permit him to aspire to the surreal. His belief finds expression in a variety of techniques that appeal to chance, of which collage is only one.

While collage may be considered a process of addition, that of *décollage* is one of subtraction. Though not widely practiced by the Surrealists, this method, described by Léo Malet in an article written for *La Conquête du Monde par l'Image,* is worth mentioning if only because Malet has made no attempt to conceal that the technique was revealed to him by chance. Décollage, too, bears out the Surrealist's confidence in purely mechanical processes, when these may be seen to have the effect of liberating the artist from preconceived and inculcated ideas. Having noticed how a poster on a wall, being torn in patches, may uncover parts of another poster beneath it, Malet was led to speculate upon the effects to be obtained by deliberately unsticking the top poster, without adopting any systematic pattern, and guided only by whim and chance. The significance of this apparently simple pastime lies of course in its exemplification of Surrealism's fidelity to the belief that man may ask of chance discoveries that could never be his without its intervention.

Better known than décollage, and just as indicative of this tendency in Surrealist thought, is Oscar Dominguez' *décalcomanie sans objet préconçu.* Decalcomania had been used in the nineteenth century, of course, but not in the way that Dominguez proposed. Instead of seeking to reproduce images already existing, Dominguez proposed to use the method of decalcomania in order to seek out images of which he would remain totally ignorant until chance had precipitated their appearance. His method, then, quite clearly rests upon the identification of chance revelation with the deepest desires of man, as Breton indeed made plain when, in the eighth number of the review *Minotaure,* where he discussed Dominguez' technique in its meaning for Surrealism, he spoke of "decalcomania of desire."

In Dominguez' form of decalcomania may be detected the double process of creation which Ernst has been careful to stress. Initially, Dominguez recommends a simply mechanical activity: gouache is spread upon a sheet of glossy paper, which is then covered with another sheet. After the sheets have been pressed together, the top one is removed and then reapplied to the lower one until the gouache has dried. Now the artist's imagination makes its contribution, stimulated by the forms before his eyes and working in collaboration with desire in the task of choosing a suitable title. Here the act of naming takes on the significance of assuming responsibility for what chance has placed in the artist's way, and which he has done no more than interpret. Since its first appearance in 1935, Dominguez' method has inspired imitation and adaptation among the Surrealist group. It has remained only for Ernst to adapt the technique to oil painting, and to produce between 1937 and 1942 a succession of landscapes that stand among his most suggestive works: *L'Ange du Marécage* (1940), *L'Europe après la Pluie* (1940–42), *Le Triomphe de l'Amour.*[4]

Meanwhile the techniques of *heatage* and *solarisation* introduced into photography by Man Ray entrusted results to chance; as did Esteban Francès' *grattage*, which resembles décollage and decalomania in its invocation of chance through mechanical means—here the arbitrary scratching of a painted surface, upon which colors have been distributed haphazardly. Like Paalen's *fumage*—the interpretation of smoke trails left when a candle flame has been brought close to a smooth surface—grattage permits of what Ernst calls "the intensification of the irritability of the mind's faculties by appropriate technical means." Here, in fact, is the advantage of the artist's invitation to chance to collaborate in artistic creation: but providing him with a sort of momentum, it augments his creative capabilities. Techniques such as those mentioned have, therefore, the signal quality of serving the Surrealist as stimulants of a special kind and potency, justifying Ernst's claim in *Beyond Painting* to have "looked on as a spectator" at the birth of certain of his pictures: "I saw with my eyes the appearances of things receding, and I felt a calm and ferocious joy. In the measure of my activity (passivity) I contributed to the general overthrow of those values which, in our time, have been considered the most established and secure."

So far as the Surrealist is concerned, willingness to submit to suggestions coming from outside—those, especially, implicit in the artistic process itself—brings rewards as inevitable as they are fortuitous. Ready co-operation with chance impels the artist to further reflection upon the nature of identity, and the means by which it may be brought to light, modified, and even transformed. The stasis of everyday existence yields to a metamorphosis that has its own vertiginous fascination.

If the Surrealist painter and photographer may hope to turn chance to account, what sort of intervention can the Surrealist expect of it when his essential materials are words? The Surrealist poet's eagerness to invoke chance is implicit in his willingness to resort to automatic writing. But this by no means proves that he may, with the same deliberateness as the painter, invite its participation. Whereas techniques calculated to provoke chance revelations suggest themselves without difficulty in plastic Surrealism, those Surrealists whose expression is purely verbal have had to break down forms of resistance to which they have been educated; just as, in automatic writing, they have had to throw off the inhibitions inherent in logical thought and expression. Indicative of the difficulty of their task, is that they have felt it useful to approach this matter through a communal activity which at first sight may seem devoid of serious intent: the practice of certain games.

But these games have proved a mixed blessing. Although evidently capable of advancing Surrealism's enquiries, their immediate effect—especially as it appears to those outside the Surrealist group—is to permit the inference that Surrealism is something of a joke, or at least mere amusement. Those wishing to discredit Surrealism, or to minimize its significance, readily find evidence suitable to their purpose in the Surrealists' use of means that appear rather frivolous, and certainly lacking in the seriousness claimed for the Surrealist mission. Yet in spite of the criticism and even mockery engendered by their advocacy of a number of quite simple games, Surrealists have persisted in proposing certain forms of play as valid methods for attaining and exploring the surreal.

The Surrealist attitude toward games is quite a precise one, and fully in keeping with the demands they make of the artist. In short, games are regarded as less a form of relaxation than an activity capable of making a valuable contribution to the attainment of the surreal. The game, according to Hans Bellmer "belongs to the category of 'experimental poetry'." Bellmer's statement is borrowed from the preface to his *Les Jeux de la Poupée* (1949), a collection of photographs (accompanied by texts by Eluard, inspired by them) of his *poupée démontable*. Bellmer's doll is anatomically rearranged and "modified" in accordance with instinctive and frequently erotic impulses on the part of the photographer. So when Bellmer draws attention to the "provocative" character of toys, he echoes certain statements made by other Surrealists regarding objects devised by them. It is significant, therefore, that Bellmer stresses that the best toy is not that with a clearly foreseeable use, but one—like his own doll—that may perpetually lead us on to the unknown. The sort of play for which it is best suited is of the kind implicit in the creation of a Surrealist collage, frottage, or decalcomania.

Like these methods of pictorial Surrealism, the game appeals to chance, and so the most characteristic Surrealist games are those designed to place the participants in a state of passivity, without which chance cannot make its full contribution. For this reason several Surrealist games focus on a purely mechanical method, readily practiced by all who are willing to join in. Best known of these is no doubt the game called *cadavre exquis*.

Exquisite Corpse takes its name from the first striking phrase produced by the Surrealists according to its rules: "le cadavre exquis boira le vin nouveau." This first example illustrates well enough the sort of results to be expected from its practice. The simplicity of the rules, the trust they reflect in collective action and the collective unconscious, and the manner in which they patently invite the revelations of chance—these are the essential and significant features of the sort of game which holds attraction for the Surrealist and permits players to compose lines like "The exquisite corpse will drink the new wine." Several people each write a noun on a piece of paper, which is then folded so as to conceal the word written. The paper is passed to a second person who adds an adjective, leaving it to a third to supply a verb, and so on. The quite fortuitous nature of this experimentation is, if anything, even more noticeable than in automatic writing, where, after all, only one mind is active at a given time. But when chance combinations prove propitious, the technique finds its vindication in phrases like these: "The Senegal oyster will eat the tricolor bread." "The twelfth century, pretty as a heart, leads off to the coal-merchant's the brain snail who politely takes off his hat." "The dormitory of friable little girls puts the odious box right." Put together by a ritual process and in a manner safeguarded from preconception and familiar relationships, phrases like these stand in protest against the world of dumb acceptance, of pedestrian associations. They deny the logic of social language, owing their vitality to the fact that chance has made them possible. Because of their strictly fortuitous origin, *cadavres exquis*, both in their verbal and in their graphic forms, affirm a liberation from habitual controls and give impetus to the imagination.

Thus the value the Surrealist sees in games of this kind is primarily an initiative one; they receive his attention as a form of "mental contagion," to borrow Ernst's phrase. Through the experience it makes possible, the *cadavre exquis* offers evidence in support of the Surrealists' contention that poetry is not the prerogative of the individual. Indeed, it is not the prerogative of man at all, but finds expression, Surrealism would have us believe, through man. This essential premise of Surrealist practice is summed up by Noël Arnaud who, in *La Conquête du Monde par l'Image* speaks pointedly of "the rich soil which belongs to all and which extends infinitely before us." Here—especially in its stress upon infinite possibility—is the idea that quite definitely separates Surrealist games from pastime, and explains the earnestness with which the Surrealists have discussed games and the results obtainable through them. The Surrealist game is deeply motivated by an urge to appeal to sources of inspiration beyond the jurisdiction of conscious thought, considered by the Surrealists to have had its day. The game reflects an aspiration to levels of the personality the mind cannot grasp or bring to light. So Breton, for example, writes in his *La Clé des Champs* (1953), "I have never experienced intellectual pleasure except on an analogical plane. For me the only *evidence* in the world is dictated by the spontaneous, extra-lucid, insolent relationship that is established in certain conditions between a certain thing and another, which common sense would prevent us from bringing face to face." What interests Breton and the Surrealists is the illumination of "relationships fruitful in a *different* way." Just as Surrealism makes use of painting, so too it wishes to make use of language. Language itself, it seems, would not exist unless it "expressed the *desire to command* which is the prerequisite condition for the act of conquest, for any act having conquest as its aim." [5] But habitual language, vitiated by social usage, has ceased to be efficacious. If it is to resume the power to command, to "break the thread of discursive thought," as Breton puts it, then it must itself be transformed. This is the transformation Surrealism proposes to effect through the discovery of a new language which will be placed at the disposal of all. Inspired by this ambition, the *cadavre exquis* probes the unknown and reports back its findings. So does the Surrealist game *Si . . . Quand.*

In *Si . . . Quand* each of a number of players writes on a piece of paper a hypothetical phrase beginning with *if* or *when*. On another he writes a proposition in the future or conditional tense. The game consists simply in bringing together one of the first phrases with one of the second. What results is a sentence containing two clauses impeccably related from the grammatical point of view, but— having been associated by a chance process acknowledging no rights in accepted logic—not satisfying to the demands of rational sequence:

If there were no guillotine
Wasps would take off their corsets.

If octopuses wore bracelets
Boats would be drawn by flies.

When aeronauts will have attained the seventh heaven
Statues will order themselves cold suppers.

The fact that statements produced in this manner are, like those we owe to *cadavres exquis*, not merely nonsensical—in the way the works of Lewis Carroll and Edward Lear are nonsensical—but amusing, in no way dimishes their value for the Surrealists, who have read Freud's *Der Witz und seine Beziehung zum Unbewussten.* That the participants in *Si . . . Quand* have only a limited control over the humorous effects they are producing—and in *cadavres exquis* no conscious control at all—matters little. For humor, to the Surrealist, is "the disinterested and direct expression of the unconscious." [6] Taking their cue from Hegel, the Surrealists welcome humor's critical potential and show themselves eager to develop it as far as they can. This is because to Marco Ristitch who speaks for Surrealism, humor is essentially "an intuitive and implicit criticism of the mental mechanism in its conventionality." Humor is consequently prized as a means of questioning conventionality and of bringing it into disrepute. The result is to remove facts from their normal context, thus, in Ristitch's phrase, "precipitating them into a vertiginous play of unexpected, surreal relationships."

The Surrealist hope of bringing the surreal into everyday experience promises realization more quickly through humor than through any other means. The Surrealist sees humor as the conjunction of the real and the fantastic: not only helping man resist the claims of the reality to which the world has accustomed him, but also placing within his reach the means to shake off habitual thought, thus permitting him to aspire to another form of reality, which answers another logic. By enabling man to cast doubt upon the validity of objective reality, humor derides the importance of this reality, and disposes of the limitations it places upon man's thinking. Humor thus helps to make Breton's vital leap feasible.

So in Surrealist hands humor becomes a weapon. And this remains the case even when the Surrealists appear to be placing this weapon in the hands of others, with the unspoken invitation to use it against Surrealism itself. The Surrealist is not unwilling to provoke laughter by what he paints pictorially or verbally. One might even say that laughter is, in Surrealism, a calculated risk. For the Surrealists know laughter to be, very often, an instinctive response to the disturbing and even to the incomprehensible —symptomatic of the individual's wish to encompass what he cannot understand, to reduce it to terms that renew his confidence in himself. This kind of laughter is frequently liberated by Surrealism. Indeed, it often becomes a means of captivating an audience, of commanding attention long enough for the serious intent, concealed by the joke, to take effect. So the Surrealists are not averse to provoking amusement through what they create, even when amusement is evidently the defense-mechanism set in motion by the spectacle of the unfamiliar. Consideration of the evidence indicates that the Surrealist usually knows in advance what our first reaction will be. His real concern is therefore our second reaction: What happens to us and to our attitude toward stable reality, once we have passed the moment of amusement at the idea of a soluble fish, or a white-haired revolver, an arthritic grasshopper or an aphrodisiac dinner-jacket?

Although it may be tempting to scoff at the Surrealists' trust in chance, to question the latter's reliability, and to feel concern at the facility risked by any artist seeking to induce its collaboration, the Surrealists themselves remain persuaded that the benefits of their methods in this form of exploration outnumber the disadvantages. The consistency of the Surrealists' attitude, in fact, renders much of the criticism which comes to mind not simply unimportant but really irrelevant. The belief in the power of the unconscious mind to bring to the surface material that satisfies man's needs, and confidence in the communicability of this material in spite of its anti-rational nature—these form only part of Surrealism's reply to objections of this kind. Exploitation of chance is, like every other technique to which the Surrealists have accorded attention, not designed to systematize methods, but to examine possible lines of approach that will hasten man's perception and comprehension of the world of the surreal. No Surrealist would expect chance to reveal something of value every time it is interrogated. But this does not diminish the significance of the revelations that do occur thanks to the methods Surrealism has proposed. Nor does it mean that those revelations which present themselves are not accepted with gratitude. On the contrary; the very uneven quality of the material made available by chance serves to remind the Surrealist that he is not primarily an artist, aiming every time to produce a masterpiece. He finds his failures as stimulating as his successes, in their reminder that his role, if he is to be effective as a Surrealist, must remain that of medium, concentrating all energies on remaining faithful to the principles imposed upon him by the acceptance of this role.

What the Surrealist offers may be laughable, but it is never irrelevant or merely whimsical. Those who give Surrealism their attention find themselves transported to a world that is sometimes frightening—as in Ernst's *Two Children Frightened by a Nightingale*, or in some of the stories of Leonora Carrington. Yet this is a strangely compelling world, where are to be encountered the fetishistic objects of Dali, or Meret Oppenheim. Here we watch the Senegal oyster eat the tricolor bread, and witness the brain snail's politeness. For the surreal, as chance makes us aware, is an irrational world.

PROSPECTING THE IMAGINARY 7

*Art and Poetry bring to light the irrational
by prospecting the imaginary.*

Simon Hantaï & Jean Schuster

Surrealism's interest in the dream world, faith in automatism and confidence in chance all point to the favor with
which it has regarded the irrational—the ultimate expression of protest against organized reality. All the techniques
so far considered have as their consequence the increased
liberation of imagination, and indicate that Surrealism
obliges the imagination to recognize allegiance to nothing
but its own desire. Instinctively, the Surrealist prefers the
irrational to the world of normality; and his instinct in this
direction finds support in the ideas his ambitions have led
him to formulate.

One of the fundamental aims of Surrealism has always
been to break certain fetters of which Breton has spoken in
Entretiens. Of these the most important is the restraint
imposed upon man by logic and the demands it makes upon
human thought. As early as 1927, in his *Introduction au
Discours sur le Peu de Réalité,* Breton spoke forthrightly of
the "peril" in which we are placed by the general application

of the dogma of reason. This text takes up the protest also publicized in its author's two manifestoes, and to which the Surrealists have returned repeatedly. In doing so, the defenders of Surrealist principles have made clear one essential point: their refusal to accept logical processes as efficacious in solving the fundamental problems of human existence.

Refusing logic, therefore, the Surrealists have turned to illogicality, in which they have seen a powerful weapon in their struggle against forces which they consider hold up man's advancement. One of the best-known spokesmen of the Surrealist attitude in this matter was Salvador Dali who, during an address at the Museum of Modern Art in New York, delivered at the end of the thirties, condemned beyond redemption "all the sordid mechanisms of logic and all mental prisons." So, as explained by Dali, the purpose of Surrealism is to "deliver the subconscious from the principle of reality." Dali's statement is important in that it goes on to indicate the reasons lying at the source of the Surrealist's impulse to deny reality as we know it: Dali speaks of "finding a source of splendid delirious images," that he evidently believes cannot be ours so long as we live by the criteria of accepted reality. Thus, if the Surrealists have ardently and unhesitatingly opposed reason, it is because they reject the constraints it engenders in favor of a liberty reflected in those splendid and delirious images of which Dali has spoken. Reason is the enemy that must be driven out, before man can hope fully to possess the surreal. And of course, the Surrealist identifies the full possession of the surreal with the full possession of the self—the final perception of the true nature of human identity. As a result, he condemns what Aragon has called in *Le Paysan de Paris* "the false duality of man" imposed upon us by reason.

The seriousness of the ambition which inspired Aragon's words and the genuine faith it occasions in the value of irrational experiences show that Surrealism's confidence in the irrational denotes something more than the simple desire to shock and scandalize. This is especially noticeable when the Surrealists' faith in the irrational is examined against the background of their wish to escape, and their belief that the form of escape they desire may best be effected through rejection of the controls associated with reason and logic. Here is a genuine instinct to reverse the order of things, to work from a standpoint quite different from that of the rational world, and to grant human imagination a freedom it cannot know until its fetters have been struck off.

The shock offered by Surrealism is one that administers a rebuff to the rational world. Surrealist distortion marks a break with the habitual and is, in consequence, a plea for the surrender of all preconceptions limiting the function and significance of things around us in a static unexciting world. This plea is formulated in terms as varied as Breton's white-haired revolver, or Dali's soft watches—objects that can be taken in the hand but not captivated, not submitted to the exigencies of a rationally ordered world. Such objects typify Surrealism's aim to make art explosive. The explosion which it occasions will clear away the old world and prepare the new. So distortion, transformation, metamorphosis—anything in fact that resists the perniciously stable nature of the universe as we know it—these are the methods the Surrealist wishes to employ to actively weaken the demands of the rational and to introduce the potentialities of the irrational.

In this way the Surrealists' interest in the irrational takes its prescribed place beside the practice of automatism as a form of protest against conservatism. Here Surrealism's artistic ambitions parallel its social protest, as Breton implied when introducing the catalogue of the 1947 International Surrealist Exhibition: "The account Surrealism has to settle with its time, on the plastic plane as elsewhere, was first of all social. It was, and still is, a matter of foiling the plot laid at every troubled moment of history and which tends jealously to make conservative forms prevail." Surrealism's deliberate exploration of the world of the irrational proves its mission to have remained unchanged: to awaken in man a new awareness which will provoke him to react against the sham and the traditional, the safe and the reasonable. It indicates Surrealism's preference for an art that may have its dangers, but which certainly has also its rewards. A belief in the relevance of these rewards to their own ambitions has led the Surrealists to approve, in principle, of anything that questions the right of conservatism to impose its controls and to hold imagination in check. Surrealism welcomes the probing of accepted practice, of whatever seems to represent stagnation rather than progress, blind acceptance rather than intelligent enquiry. And it has never been reluctant, when this seemed necessary, to require and propose radical revision.

Breton's *Second Manifesto of Surrealism* postulates that the belief that some things *exist* while others *do not* is "a cancer." This is the cancer upon which the Surrealists have felt it most urgent to operate. The result has been a continued stress upon the necessity for suprise both in painting and in literature; surprise being regarded as a means well suited to bringing man to that state of grace towards which Surrealism is oriented. Thus, according to Breton's *La Position politique du Surréalisme,* the essential quality of art resides in imagination alone: "This is to say *everything depends upon the liberty with which this imagination succeeds in producing itself and only itself."* The complete freedom granted the imagination in Surrealism, and the importance Breton attaches to the fact that human imagination owes nothing to the world outside man, point up the reasons that have endowed the irrational with so much prestige for the Surrealists.

So Surrealism's use of surprise and distortion may be considered as intended to utilize imagination in such a way as to introduce man to the world of the irrational, where the Surrealist proposes to seek that freedom usually denied him. Yet formulated in these terms, Surrealism's faith in the irrational might seem to denote an instinct for evasion of a kind quite foreign to Surrealist practice. It is necessary therefore to consider in what way the Surrealists' use of techniques to invoke the irrational may be said to constitute a step along the road they have chosen, and to establish the precise meaning attaching in Surrealism to the word "irrational."

Simon Hantaï and Jean Schuster have taken great care to distinguish between the irrational and the unreal. For them, the irrational is that which *"exists* and *is becoming."* [1] To the degree that these words may be regarded as representing the view of the Surrealists in general, they may be considered proof that Surrealism's exploration of the irrational has nothing to do with simple escapism. It by no means represents neglect, even momentary neglect, of their declared purpose:—to modify man's outlook and the world in which he finds himself today. Because the irrational "is becoming," it possesses vital relevance for Surrealism's ambitions. For, as Hantaï and Schuster put it, "the imaginary and the irrational tend toward the real and rational . . . the irrational of yesterday is the rational of today." So Surrealism's appeal to irrationality is evidence of persistent optimism in the face of depressing reality. And the Surrealists' attitude in this matter betokens a conviction that, thanks to the lessons to be learned from the irrational, man may hope to see Surrealism vindicate its claim to be a form of *action,* when he sees the world changed in accordance with his desires.

This same conviction has dictated the Surrealists' response to the work of certain creative artists—especially within their own group—in whom they detect aspirations of which they approve. Of Jindrich Styrsky, Benjamin Péret wrote in the catalogue *Surrealist Intrusion in the Enchanters' Domain:* "In Styrsky's work, nothing *is* but everything can *become,* since it is situated at the place where the wind is born that is going to swell the sails or unroof the houses at the same time as it creates, here, impending floods, there, rich crops." The manner in which Péret's words echo those of Hantaï and Schuster will not escape notice. Like them, Péret reveals the criteria by which Surrealism judges

achievement. Styrsky's irrational, it is therefore worth
noting, is not set apart from life and is not without bearing
upon existence in this world. It tends towards action, as the
Surrealists use the word when speaking of art as they wish
to see it practiced—at once destructive and creative: destroying the old world but also creating the new; proving the
instability of the former and the possibility of bringing the
latter into our experience. In this way, the irrational of
Surrealism offers no cheap relief from the world about us,
except in so far as it implicates us, by showing what can be,
opposing it to what already exists, and indicating that it is
already becoming. Here lies the true revolutionary function
of art, as the Surrealists conceive it. It lies in the combination of our world with that other world the artist has the
privilege of revealing. Here is that vital spark for which
Surrealism searches and which Edouard Jaguer, writing in
The Enchanters' Domain, detects in the work of Corneille,
whose paintings, he remarks, "express with serenity his
decision to elicit the truth of every possible *concrete development,* hidden from our numbed perception by the multiple
circuits of *existence* and *vision,* free to wander out aimlessly
in a fan-like stampede of colours."

The transformation of vision, the transposition of existence—Surrealism has never wearied in its hope to effect
these results. It has never betrayed any reluctance to follow
paths promising the rewards it has sought. Quoting Péguy's
reference to Descartes as "ce chevalier français qui partait
d'un si bon pas," Nora Mitrani has affirmed, "But to the
French chevalier Descartes, we prefer the Percivals who,
with heart full of anguish, plunge into the black woods, in
search of the impossible." [2] Where Breton speaks of a state
of grace, Nora Mitrani invokes the theme of the Holy Grail.
The significance of their imagery is clear enough, and gives
meaning to a note on Yves Laloy in *The Enchanters' Domain,* signed by Victor Bounoure, who tells us that Laloy's
pictures are characterized by "the aggressiveness by which
alone the inner vision is attained. Each is the signal of a
victory over the opacity of the perceptible décor, the sover-

eign result of a new and perilous adventure." Discovery,
linked with the aggressiveness Surrealism learned from
Dada, is here associated quite plainly with the attainment of
an inner vision that cannot be achieved without a searching
exploration of the self, a deeper perception of personal identity. So Laloy, commands the respect of his fellows for helping to advance the cause of revolt. Through works like his we
may hope to appreciate the pertinence of Maddox' prophesy,
made in the final number of *London Bulletin:* "It does not
seem impractical to us to organize a system by which it
would be possible to discredit completely the trophies of the
rational world of things and happenings."

If we are to believe Aragon, of course, the ambition of
which Maddox speaks has most chance of realization
through verbal images rather than through pictorial ones.
In *Le Paysan de Paris,* he writes, "The vice called *Surrealism* is the unreasoning and impassioned use of the stupi-
fying image, for itself and for what it brings with it, in the
domain of representation by way of unforeseeable perturba-
tion and metamorphosis: for each image, every time, forces
you to revise the universe." Thus, as Breton has confided in
Du Surréalisme en ses Œuvres vives (1953), the attitude
Surrealism toward nature is dictated above all by its concept
of the poetic image—the linking of unrelated realities in a
manner possible only when all critical sense has been surrendered. Surrealism calls upon its public to witness a form
of unreasonable confrontation because it believes that illumination can come only in the absence of reason. So there is no
cause to question the Surrealist painter's ability to emulate
the discoveries of the poet. The painter Max Walter Svanberg is quite emphatic in *The Enchanters' Domain:* "Total,
disquieting and ambiguous beauty can be achieved only
through the irrational game of perpetual figuration, poetic
and liberating, wherein lines and colours cease to be absolute
aims to become means of increasing the intensity of the
imagination." The perpetual figuration to which Svanberg
refers is then reminiscent of the metamophosis dear to
Masson, or the infinite suggestiveness from which the paint-

ings of Miró grow. It stands for the same resistance to
immobility to be encountered in their work, and draws
strength from the same source: an imagination liberated
from rational control.

In his *The Conquest of the Irrational,* Dali claimed his sole
ambition to be "to materialize with the most imperialistic
rage for precision the images of concrete irrationality." We
have his word that, to him, what counts is the subject "in its
concrete irrationality," the means of pictorial expression
being simply "placed at the service of this subject." What is
significant for Surrealism is that the images of which Dali
speaks are, in his own words, "authentically unknown images," no more familiar to the painter himself than to the
public seeing them for the first time. In his *Secret Life of
Salvador Dali* (1948), Dali has related how he decided to
undertake a picture in which he proposed to scrupulously
reproduce images as they presented themselves to him, admitting no order beyond that dictated by automatism: "I
would follow only my pleasure, my most uncontrollable bio-
logical desire." His imagination disengaged from all
restraint, he confined his attention to transposing onto canvas the images released in this manner.

Possible objections to such a method are met in Dali's
affirmation: "The fact that I myself, at the moment of painting, do not understand the significance of my pictures cannot mean that my pictures have no meaning; on the contrary
their meaning is so profound, complex, coherent, involun-
tary, that it escapes mere analysis by logical intuition."
Considered apart from certain pronouncements by Tanguy,
Ernst and Miró, Dali's words would seem merely provocative. But the apparent paradox of his statement is resolved
when its fidelity to Surrealist attitudes is recognized. He was
entitled to say that his Surrealist pictures can be analyzed
only a posteriori—"when the picture exists as a phenomenon." For, in doing so, he revealed that his role was that of

any authentic Surrealist, who is a medium permitting the communication of certain discoveries, projected in such a form as to retain their representative value. During the act of creation, the Surrealist has no time to wonder how readily accessible his work will prove to be. It is not his function, either, to speculate upon the meaning it may have for the public, once it is before them. If such issues were permitted to claim his attention, they would risk interfering with the flow of inspiration, check it, or divert it somewhat. His inspiration would certainly be less pure in its expression, less disinterested. If the Surrealist is to remain true to his purpose, he will be wiser to follow the example of Breton, appealing in *Nadja* to "the great quickening sonorous unconscious."

In works produced by such means as these, ideas may certainly be present. But they are necessarily linked with direct vision, as this vision reflects the artist's imaginative faculties. So, though there can be no concern for the readiness with which the public is to penetrate the meaning embodied in the created work, it is not a matter, either, of wilful esotericism, or insensitive indifference. Despite what its unfavorable critics may have said, Surrealism, even when it prospects the imaginary, is by no means but the blind elaboration of a private vocabulary, meaningful only to its inventors. Paradoxically perhaps, the Surrealists' unwillingness to over-simplify the problems of communication is indicative of responsibility, not of irresponsibility—a sign of the authenticity of their work.

Even when exploring the world of the irrational, the Surrealist is interrogating nature, searching for the very rhythm of life. He believes no better method of discovering this rhythm exists than the exercise of imagination, freed from the restraints of reason and convention. And, in Surrealism, it should never be forgotten, the imaginary is identified with the irrational. Positing a freedom the everyday world cannot know, the imaginary permits the Surrealists to "crystallize time and space in images that can only be evaluated beyond all reasonable measure, by the light of that sensibility alone which must one day or another conquer the entire realm allotted to solemn 'reason.' " [3] Without the support it draws from Surrealism's faith in an inevitable conquest over rationality, the imaginary would not be invested with the prestige the Surrealists attach to it. So the corrosive power of the Surrealist image, in both poetry and painting, attacks reason and conformism, and derives its liberating energy from this fact.

In proposing, as Georges Hugnet phrases it, to investigate *"the immense undetermined region over which reason does not extend its protectorate,"* [4] the Surrealists follow on after all those writers and painters who have shared Guy de Maupassant's view that "only madmen are happy, because they have lost the feeling of reality." It is therefore particularly relevant that the *Manifesto of Surrealism* already speaks in 1924 of the lessons to be learned from deranged states, when Breton confesses that he could happily spend his whole life provoking the confidences of the insane—just as he was later to do in *Nadja.* In 1928, he and Aragon published a tract "La Cinquantaine de l'Hystérie," in which they celebrated the fiftieth anniversary of Charcot's pioneer work in the field of hysteria, hailed by them as "the greatest poetic discovery of the XIXth century." With notable frequency since that date, articles have appeared in Surrealist reviews to commemorate the artistic productions of certain individuals whom society has judged unbalanced. Meanwhile Surrealist painters like Ernst have admitted to a particular interest in insane art, and avowed its influence upon their own work, at least during certain periods.

The immediate appeal of insane art to a group intent upon revolutionizing the verbal and pictorial image is easily imagined. But Surrealism's respect for madness takes them beyond that general esteem which, we are reminded in André Malraux's *Les Voix du Silence,* our period feels for this "sort of second sight and liberation." It takes us further, too, than the nostalgia Charles Lamb betrayed in a letter to Coleridge, in which he wrote of the revelations made him during moments of derangement, and declared: "Dream not, Coleridge, of having tasted all the grandeur and wildness of fancy until you have gone mad! All now seems to me vapid, comparatively so." For when one recalls how Nerval refused to admit his insanity to be illness and his return to the world of the normal to be a cure, one comprehends what Breton meant when he referred to insane art's "reservoir of moral health." [5] To the Surrealist, insanity guarantees authenticity of a kind lacking in contemporary art, for he believes, with Breton, that it is only at the point where human reason loses control that "the most profound emotion of our being has every chance of finding expression."

Thus Surrealism's preoccupation with the question of true identity lends pertinence to its interest in insanity, which it relates to its belief that certain methods of approach are particularly adapted to revealing man to himself. Considered from this angle, the Surrealist irrational is to be regarded less as a purely selfish rejection of society than as an attempt to bring man to the threshold of a deeper comprehension of the functioning of the human mind, such as cannot be attained if attention is confined to rationally recognizable evidence. The profound emotion of which Breton speaks is, as he emphasizes, quite unsuited for projection within the framework of the so-called real world, which must cease to command man's respect, if he is to make progress in the direction Surrealism indicates.

The operative word is "recognition." For Surrealism remains a search, undertaken by the artist through the experience of the irrational. Therefore Surrealism cannot take its full effect until the public has made the contribution demanded of it through a sense of involvement. In the world of the irrational, to which insanity furnishes one of the keys, man is introduced to a universe in which he may try out his knowledge of himself, testing the limitations of this knowledge and pushing them back, as he gains confidence in his capacities, and finally learns what identity is.

There is no denying that insanity is the privilege of relatively few persons. In recognizing this fact, the Surrealists have not omitted to stress that hallucination may be experienced by many more individuals, especially when they feel inclined to do so. "In the final analysis," Breton wrote in *Point du Jour*, "everything depends upon our power of voluntary hallucination." And Jean Cazaux remarked in the eleventh number of *Minotaure* that "poetic knowledge of the world is above all *hallucinatory*." No wonder, then, that the Surrealists have devoted much attention to devising and adapting methods for inducing the form of hallucination that interests them: "It must be admitted that when there is a total confusion between the real image and the hallucination it has provoked, no misunderstanding is possible." [6]

The Surrealist poet, whatever his chosen form of expression, is, as Eluard puts it, *halluciné par excellence*, whether he deliberately seeks to induce hallucination or no. Some, like the painter Miró, find it difficult to speak of their work, because, as in his case, "it is always born in a state of hallucination, provoked by some shock or other, objective or subjective," for which they must disclaim responsibility.[7] For others, hallucinatory impressions may present themselves without warning, and in unexpected places:

The real has glass barriers and gazing ahead I see
an ended gangway going up into the night
pens with people on either side paired: and alone
through the still images eating them shade by shade
lamps lurch in a row swung from the middle of the
    road.[8]

But whatever their origin, the images generated in hallucination resemble those provoked by automatism: they do not need to be rationally explicable to communicate a message. Communication in such cases depends upon the degree to which artist and public participate in the collective unconscious from which the Surrealist irrational draws strength.

So Dali, in a "Declaration of the Independence of the Imagination and the Rights of Man to his own Madness," could affirm "All men are equal in their madness," and see in madness the common basis of the human spirit. Here, indeed, is Dali's authority for deliberately undertaking to adapt and adopt means made possible by insanity for the exploration of the irrational. Thanks to Dali's example, insanity and hallucination ceased to be for Surrealism merely a source of encouragement to become valuable technical devices.

Because of Dali's gift for publicity—and especially for self-publicity—his proposal of a paranoiac method has contributed to a notable degree in fostering a widespread view that Surrealism and insanity are one. As a result, little or no attempt has been made to show that it was the generally agreed belief among Surrealists in the efficacy of hallucination which led Dali to stress the inspirational value of paranoia. Consequently, it has not been sufficiently emphasized that the insanity of which he speaks from the Surrealist standpoint is not the apparently aimless wandering of a deranged mind, unwilling to face reality. It represents, rather, an intentional denial of that reality, as the artist seeks for renewed comprehension. So Dali's paranoia is "a delirium of interpretation implying a systematic structure." Dali does not, any more than his fellow Surrealists, conceal that distortion, metamorphosis and the unexpected displacement of objects and phenomena are essential to his method, and that they tend more toward the world of the irrational than toward the realities about us.

Thus, far from acknowledging the primacy of these realities, Dali's celebrated article, "L'Ane pourrissant," in the first number of *Le Surréalisme au service de la Révolution* (1930), declares that the very images of reality depend upon "the degree of our paranoiac faculty." So, a person endowed sufficiently with this faculty may see the form of an object taken from reality assume successive changes, all dictated, it should be noted, by his desire. What is more, these transformations are not solely subject to the control of the observer—the artist himself—but recognizable to everyone to whom the paranoiac has revealed them. No more dramatic assertion of the common basis of desire could be found than this, which Dali has substantiated in several paintings in which forms—building up a human figure, perhaps—are simultaneously arranged to create a scene, thus communicating an inescapable impression of two pictures existing in one, and at the same time. These pictures are mutually dependent to such a point that, while wishing to look at one of them, the spectator cannot completely disregard the other. Simple as this form of visual play is, it takes its part in Surrealism's attack upon fixed and rigid reality, such as is found also in the images of Surrealist verse. Hence Dali's confession of faith: "I believe the moment is at hand when, by a paranoiac and active process of the mind, it will be possible (simultaneously with automatism and other passive states) to systematize confusion and to contribute to discrediting completely the world of reality."

Dali's words make clear why, despite the fact it has had so few exponents, his paranoiac method has occupied an honorable place among the techniques of revolt promoted by Surrealism. Its use is motivated by aims readily assimilated to the Surrealists' highest ambitions, and the tendencies it exemplifies have become familiar: reality is *utilized* by the imagination, now released, thanks to the methods employed, from rational control, obliged to take account of no criteria beyond those proposed by man's desire. Surrealism's persistent determination to trust passivity lends special meaning to the paranoiac method—acknowledged by Dali himself as making its appeal directly to the unconscious. So he declares the images of paranoiac thought will not merely spring from the unconscious, but their paranoiac power will itself be at the service of the conscious. Domination of reality, not submission to its control—here is the prize Dali believes may be won through the irrational, no less than through automatism, or appeals to chance.

The paranoiac method, in consequence, does more than reaffirm what Surrealism hopes to learn through automatism and similar practices. Through paranoia, the Surrealist may confidently turn inward rather than outward. He may thus hope to invalidate the stability of reality, not merely by denying it, but by making reality itself serve his purpose. So Dali's form of protest is more subtle than it might be assumed to be. Here, reality is less rejected than assimilated to a quite remarkable degree. So the method Dali's showmanship soon led him to debase still commands the respect of the Surrealists, whose leader has never denied or under-estimated the appropriateness of the paranoiac method to Surrealism's ambitions. And Breton has expressed particular indulgence also for the paranoiac-critical method, originating with Dali.

As defined by Dali himself, the paranoiac-critical method strikingly evidences Surrealism's refusal to be bounded by the rational, and its appeal to the irrational. Through this activity, Dali attempted to show to what degree paranoia is "a mental crisis" of the greatest significance for Surrealism. He was concerned, he has explained, with "a spontaneous method of *irrational knowledge* based upon the critical and systematic objectification of delirious associations and interpretations," that would permit him to "explain" paintings executed by other painters in terms that proved sometimes to be as alarming as they were novel. Thus his method made it possible for him to discover in the apparently innocuous works of Millet—that "immeasurably misunderstood painter"—a recurrent eroticism hidden beneath the innocent surface of pictures like *L'Angélus*. Needless to say, the associations and interpretations liberated during Dali's examination of such works came, as he stressed, from irrational knowledge—an understanding not obtainable by rational means, and serving ends quite outside reason and logic. Faithful to the essence of paranoia, Dali's critical method made use of the reality of the picture before him, and proceeded to transform it according to his desires, and in a manner suggestive of the way in which many of the Surrealist objects should be viewed.

Fascinated as they have been by found objects, the Surrealists have not been satisfied to rely solely upon chance to establish contact between themselves and the reality they have undertaken to transform. Very frequently, they have modified these objects by a form of "correction" highly significant in its implications. Then, too, they have created objects of their own, in a variety of shapes and a wide range of materials. The enigmatic character presented by such objects has the effect of interrogating the spectator, after the manner of Paalen's painting. In some cases, indeed, one may conclude these objects to have been placed before us in order to irritate and disturb, in a manner reminiscent of that which we associate with Dadaist objects. But the more interesting examples are those embodying a meaning which, if not readily perceptible, may be revealed to us by our instinctive, irrational response to their strange appeal. Interrogation by the Surrealist object—effected through the shock it administers to the imagination—then becomes self-interrogation: as we come in contact with these objects, we learn something about ourselves.

The list would be a long one, if we wished to include all those Surrealists who have joined in the creation of irrational objects, particularly favored by Breton. The value attaching to them is proportional to their expression of Surrealism's refusal to be bound by reality. They open our eyes to a whole range of physical phenomena that could exist for us if rational sense did not deny them life. In challenging the world of conventional relationships, they objectify human desire in terms with which the Surrealists have sought to familiarize their public. An initial impression of shock sets in motion a feeling of liberation and revelation, closely related to a sense of penetration to the irrational. In many cases humor is made to discredit the habitual and to show its limitations to be illusory. So here is a reminder of Breton's announcement in the first *Manifesto* that, for Surrealism, it is essential to release language from what he calls the sclerosis traceable to logical thought.

At this point we are prepared to appreciate the importance the Surrealists attach to verbal experimentation designed to discover and make available a new kind of language. Representative of these experiments is the series of exercises in composition culminating in the volume Breton and Eluard published in 1930, under the significant title *L'Immaculée Conception*. The immaculate conception of which these authors speak is the production of texts without the intervention of logic and beyond the confines of rational preconceptions. Thus *L'Immaculée Conception* stood for an attempt to enrich the field of discovery opened up by automatic writing: an attempt unhesitatingly taking as its point of departure the irrational.

When *L'Immaculée Conception* appeared, it was announced as an exposition of the "latent content" of Surrealism, to complement the "manifest content" expressed in the *Manifesto of Surrealism*. Among the texts collected in the volume were the results of experiments undertaken in an attempt to simulate states of delirium, mental debility, dementia praecox, and even general paralysis. These were all offered under the revealing subtitle "Les Possessions," to show that the author's wish was to assume once more a role very like that of the medium: to become a sort of bridge between mankind and the subliminal message. In his preamble to this section, Breton demonstrated his fidelity to the major preoccupations of Surrealism, when he spoke of the wish to "reduce the antinomy or reason and madness." So the aim that inspires the composition of this part of *L'Immaculée Conception* as the Surrealists have taught us to expect, had nothing to do with literature or with the production of picturesque effects. The authors' purpose was rather to indicate, as the preamble states, that a normal man, "trained poetically," can reproduce the most paradoxical verbal manifestations: that he may assume delirious ideas at will. Breton therefore confided that he and Eluard hoped the results they had obtained and were now placing before the public would hasten the break-down of those separate categories into which men are divided in such a way as to set apart "those who have an account to settle with reason," defined as that which "daily denies us the right to express ourselves by means that are instinctive to us." In this consists the value of the experiment in question: "We have become conscious, in ourselves, of resources that until now could not be suspected." So *L'Immaculée Conception* represented at the same time an advance along the path of self-discovery, and the true revelation of identity, as well as the release of poetic sources of unsuspected power.

Surrealism's interest in the irrational reflects a need to evade consecrated forms and fixed patterns of thought, experience and creativity. But, important though this impulse is, it does not fully show the extent of the faith the Surrealists have placed in irrationality. Something of this is indicated, however, in Crevel's *Le Clavecin de Diderot:* "We shall be content with working for an end of the Immobile." Surrealism's appeal to the irrational is an offshoot of this ambition, and accompanies a fundamental desire to achieve fuller understanding and development, believed possible only through a deeper examination of the human mind in its imaginative activity. The important words are transformation, not evasion; revolution, not escapism. Thus, in Surrealism, the irrational is not so much the avoidance of the real as the projection of desire, the wish to change the real, and, at the same time, man's view of himself. The readiness with which the Surrealists have responded to the irrational and turned to it for inspiration is a token of their continued need for radical change, which has brought still further consequences.

THE ENCHANTERS' DOMAIN 8

*The marvellous, heart and nervous system
of all poetry.* Benjamin Péret

In his *Aragon surréaliste,* André Gavillet tentatively suggests that the instinct for the marvellous, so characteristic of the Surrealists, may perhaps be detected already in the various excursions projected by the Dadaists.[1] It is indeed true that Aragon, one of those most eager to organize those excursions in 1920, was later to write *Le Paysan de Paris* (1926), in which he displayed a remarkable gift for discovering the marvellous behind everyday reality. But whatever the origins of Surrealism's interest in the marvellous, and whatever contribution Aragon may have made to its development, this interest is so noticeable that at least one critic, Marcel Béalu, has equated Surrealism with "the aspiration as old as the world, toward the fantastic, the bizarre, the marvellous." [2] Certainly, Béalu's generalization is provisonally acceptable if the word "fantastic" is given the sense proposed by Hermann Voss in the catalogue of an exhibition, "Bosch, Goya et le Fantastique," held in Bordeaux in 1957: "We speak of 'fantastic' in the narrow sense of the term when the artist's imagination, abandoning the traditional paths of religious Faith or of the Myth, moves outside all limitations of this order with sovereign liberty, but equally when the objective, faithful restitution of our everyday life becomes a surreality, as in the creations of a Dali or a Max Ernst."

Taking these words as starting point, one sees without difficulty the great attraction the marvellous exerts upon the Surrealist mind. For in no aspect of Surrealism more than in its attitude towards the marvellous is one aware of the extent to which the Surrealists seek to modify reality, to deny its restrictive laws, and to permit it a liberty at present unknown.

Michel Carrouges, discussing what drew him toward Surrealism, has confessed, "Surrealism was the revelation of the presence and power of the marvellous, the destruction of positivist conceptions of the world," [3] thus making clear that, in Surrealism, advocacy of the marvellous is closely linked with a general attitude towards reality and the world about man. If, to quote Breton's "Limites non Frontières du Surréalisme," [4] the Surrealists "throw themselves headlong into the marvellous," it is because they have the highest hopes of what it may reveal to them. Asked what they have sought to put in place of all they have tried to destroy, Breton answered without hesitation, in *Entretiens* (1952), "the appetite for the marvellous, of course."

In following the promise of the marvellous, Surrealism has remained consistent with itself and true to its principles: summed up in an instinctive desire for discovery and revelation from which increased understanding must result. The Surrealists' identification of the marvellous with progress is to be noticed from the first *Manifesto,* in which Breton writes that the marvellous is always beautiful: "any marvellous is beautiful, indeed only the marvellous is beautiful." Here is the explanation for Surrealism's behavior before the marvellous, so well prepared by its attitude towards chance, automatism, and the irrational. The marvellous, to borrow Aragon's phrase in *Le Paysan de Paris,* is "the contradiction appearing in the real." Hence its potency for the Surrealist, and his belief in the necessity for "perpetual complicity with enchantments," [5] in opposition to those ideas that separate man from a full comprehension of the universe, in the light of the surreal and under the guidance of desire: the aim remains the same—to destroy the antinomies which the Surrealists, Breton at their head, have attacked so violently.

There should be nothing surprising then in Breton's declaration that the marvellous is "the sole source of eternal communication between men." [6] The marvellous takes the place, in Surrealism, of divine providence. Its prestige is limitless, and gives point to the Surrealists' use of techniques appealing to chance and to automatism. "In this invasion of reality by the marvellous," comments André Pieyre de Mandiargues, "rises a very vast country in which the witness, skilful enough to observe the phantasmagoric elements without frightening them off by too much attention, will be able to walk with profit." [7]

In his *L'Evidence poétique* (1937) Eluard has announced that once man attains the reality that is his right, "he will have only to close his eyes for the doors of the marvellous to open." With this promise before them, the Surrealists have asked themselves what methods will enable them to open these doors most easily and with the least delay. Delimiting the problem with useful precision, Mabille asks in the review *Arson* (1942):

Where does the marvellous reign? Is it the creative power of the mind of man; has the latter only to bring it into consciousness, express it, give it form, at first poetic, then plastic, finally make concrete objects of it? Does it belong to the external world? And are we ordinarily incapable of comprehending it for lack of keenness in our senses numbed by the habits of daily life? Is it not at once within a being and outside him, like a higher plane belonging to a wider reality which would only meet the ordinary plane of existence in narrow zones of contact, exceptional points of intersection, and turn every correspondence to special states of mind or to singular circumstances? I will retain this image, the widest; it induces us to prospect the breaches which these explosive contacts open in the walls of our sensibility.

Mabille's reference to prospecting breaches in the wall of human sensibility is clearly indicative of the role the marvellous plays in inciting the Surrealists to negate the claims of accepted reality. Thus their efforts will be concentrated upon effecting the explosive contacts of which he speaks.

The Surrealists were not slow to realize that the surest link with the marvellous is provided by the imagination. We find Svanberg for instance stressing how essential the imagination is to the Surrealist painter: "The necessary foundations of plastic art for me are a possessed, visionary, active imagination and a tyrannical need to create, its representations endowed with a particular life of its own, stimulating the imagination." [8] The painter's imagination—which, it goes without saying, resembles in this the poet's imagination—is the concrete expression of what Svanberg calls "explosive forces accumulating in the subconscious." And, of course, the form of imagination in question is "the imagination of desire," that José Pierre has called "the most faithful and most ambitious mirror of man." [9]

Surrealism's conception of the imagination is integrated with the general ambitions that prompt and govern its attitude towards art and literature and gives the fantastic a special value for the Surrealists. "The admirable thing about the fantastic," remarked Herbert Read quoting Breton, "is that it is no longer fantastic; there is only the real." [10]

Read makes a point which often has received particular emphasis in Surrealist writings. This point has received special attention in Breton's *La Clé des Champs* (1953), where Surrealism's refusal to admit the marvellous to be deprived of communication with life is unequivocally stated. Though, at present, reality and the marvellous may seem to be separated by what he calls a "sluice-gate," Breton assures us that this may be removed. This is why Surrealism is especially sympathetic toward those who have contributed to undermining all that intervenes between man and the marvellous. It singles out for approval those artists of whom Victor Bounoure has spoken in *Surrealist Intrusion in the Enchanters' Domain:* "In sharp contrast with the artists who entrusted their 'message' to a sad quantity of adequate words, other artists—who did not consider themselves as such—were bent on using words and shapes in an attempt to modify, if only for a moment, their relations with the universe."

It is worth noting that Bounoure, in this context, was speaking principally of primitive artists. For we cannot but notice that the objects of primitive art are very often specifically *magic* objects, and magic—to quote Breton's *L'Art magique* (1957)—"presupposes protestation, revolt even." The primitive artist resembles the surrealist in his pride that comes from belief that it is not God but man who disposes—or may aspire to do so. So the Surrealist is drawn to the objects of primitive art in which he sees above all the assumption by the artist of divine prerogatives. Art, for the primitive and for the Surrealist, typifies man's assertion of liberty in the face of forces threatening to overthrow him. And, in paying tribute to the magical significance of artistic creation, the Surrealists have not neglected to recognize the magical role of language.

In *La Clé des Champs* Breton draws this parallel between mystic and poetic analogy: "Poetic analogy has this in common with mystic analogy that it transgresses the law of deduction to make the mind apprehend the interdependence of two objects of thought situated on different planes, between which the logical functioning of the mind is unlikely to build a bridge and which is opposed *a priori* to any bridge at all being built." Thus, though the Surrealist dismisses any possible religious value in analogical play, Breton does emphasize that the most exciting word available to man is the word *like*, because "through it the imagination gives itself, and the highest destiny of the mind is played out." In Surrealism, indeed, the stress is upon the revolutionary value of analogical language, as it is discussed by Maddox in the review *Free Unions* (1946) : "Through our knowledge of the process of affective reaction, the image, evoked from the very source of the marvellous and put at the service of desire, becomes the means by which we seek to establish our claim to speak in the name of an authentic revolutionary art." The image is, in Surrealism, calculated to plumb the depths of the unconscious, and not to make man turn his back upon this world in favor of an afterlife in which the Surrealists refuse to believe.

It is here that the magical function of language comes to the fore. Mabille in his book *Le Merveilleux* (1946), noting—after Mallarmé—how words become debased in society, claims for them still "an obscure link" with exterior reality. They continue to "participate in the essence of things," and so provide man with "a direct and magical means of action." Pursuing Mabille's thought further, Arpad Mezei has shown the word to be "a multidimensional construction," adding, "the interchangeability of reality and language, by reason of the multidimensional nature of words, is the basis and principal key to all hermetic activity." [11]

Attention to the magical value Surrealism detects in language permits a better understanding of Mabille's definition of the marvellous as summing up for man "the possibilities of contact between what is within him and what is outside him." But little of what Mabille and his fellow-Surrealists have said on this subject would hold much meaning if it did not betray their hope of prospecting the marvellous, not only for themselves but for all men. The vitality of the marvellous in Surrealism lies in its being, as *La Clé des Champs* puts it, "the sole source of eternal communication between all men." We are returned to one of the recurrent thoughts nourishing Surrealism: the conviction, expressed by Eluard, that "poems always have big margins, big white margins of silence in which ardent memory is consumed to re-create a delirium that has no past. Their principal quality is not to evoke but to inspire." [12] Gascoyne has made the same point, but more directly:

> The armchair turned into a palace,
>   the carpet became a bank
> of withered flowers, *and it was*
> *time to go.* Every semblance
> of that which has gone before
> becomes the means by which you
> ascended the great staircase
> and took your place among the stars. [13]

Sometimes the Surrealist poet expresses a desire for insight into the world of the marvellous, as in Breton's "L'Aigrette." [14] But more often Surrealist poetry offers the unquestioning acceptance of a marvellous relationship that the poet is already experiencing, when as in Breton's "Vigilance," he "holds the thread":

> today is the day when the streets are full of hearses
> and when women cover their ring finger with pieces of
>   silk
> and the doors fall off their hinges in ruined cathedrals
> when hosts of white birds fly across the ocean from
>   america
> and pavements of cities are covered with needles
> the reservoirs are full of human hair
> fumes of sulphur envelop the houses of ill-fame
> out of which bloodred lilies appear. [15]

Such glad acceptance of a world outside of normal controls is very characteristic of certain Surrealist apocalyptic writing, in which the calmness with which the marvellous vision is received betrays aspirations those living contentedly in this world of ours would find it difficult to share.

Gascoyne's poem "Salvador Dali" closes with the spectacle of lovers floating down a cliffside like rain, after introducing its readers to a universe in which are present unmistakable erotic overtones reminiscent of the painting of Dorothea Tanning and of the stories of Leonora Carrington. Through Surrealist products like these one learns that "if appearances are not as simple as they seem, this is due to a unique kind of distraction which, here, gives access to the daily magic." [16] Distraction—denial of the restraints of the logical world—is a refusal, in the Surrealist, to accept the real as resistent to transformation. It takes him, then, beyond mere inattention or indifference, and becomes one of his means for the fuller possession of the marvellous, and, consequently, of the fuller possession of himself.

Noting in the "Dreams" number of *Cahiers GLM* that the elements of matter possess a system of valencies that orients their combination and renders certain compounds possible, while others are not, Mabille pauses to wonder if we may not expect to find artistic images brought together in a similar manner—that is, in response to qualities within the artist. That Mabille's is a proposition of persistent fascination in Surrealism is demonstrated in Breton's remark that the Surrealist's dream is "a dream of *mediation*." And so, interrogating the marvellous with this preoccupation in mind, the Surrealist finds himself obliged to reflect both upon the universe and upon man's relation to it. He discovers the world of his imagination really exists and no longer permits him to accept without question the values by which he has been accustomed to judge existence in the world outside him. "That which we used to call very proudly 'our education' needs to be begun once again, from top to bottom," explains Crevel.[17] The whole question of what exists and what does not needs to be restated with unexpected urgency; and there is no guarantee that the answer will be the one society expects:

The sun rose on a news scene, a landscape composed of
    thimbles

and darning wool, thimbles and thimbles, millions of them,
shining white in the dew, as far as the eye could reach,
    and,
populated here and there with fuse boxes inhabited by a
species of birds' eggs, pale and delicate creatures.
    I spoke to
one or two, but hadn't the heart to learn their language,
    They
would never have believed I existed.[18]

As these lines intimate, it is we who are on the outside and
who need to learn new ways of communication. By our own
fault, we are deprived of means to contact the marvellous, so
that we cannot derive from it all that we might. The jolt
administered to man's mental complacency is salutary, as
René Magritte implies when he writes: "One uses familiar
words to give a title to images, but the words cease to be
familiar when one attempts to entitle the images of resemblance." [19]

According to Paalen, Magritte "*associates* in a purely
practical way." This is to say he "*transposes* images of
objects, transporting them unchanged exactly in the manner
in which a poet uses words." [20] So one may say that
Magritte's use of visual images has the same magical significance as the Surrealist poet's use of verbal images:
"The value of art," Magritte has remarked, "is in proportion
to its power of liberating revelation." [21] Thus when E. L. T.
Mesens notes that Magritte has "pursued 'mystery' to its
dialectical conclusion: the 'non-mystery,' the poetic matter-
of fact," [22] he uncovers the secret of the surface innocence of
Magritte's painting. Here is a painter who can call a canvas
depicting a pipe *Ce n'est pas une Pipe*, because he is concerned to transcribe "visible poetic images," analogous to
the thimbles in Sewter's poem. Magritte makes us aware
that the apparent resemblance his objects bear to the habitual objects about us is an illusion. Writing in 1959,
Magritte confided that his attitude towards his art corre-
sponds to his feeling of "the mystery of the familiar world in

which we live." [23] His attitude is, therefore, typical of those
Surrealists who have turned to the marvellous for inspiration and discovery. Its interest for them is closely linked
with their desire to act upon reality. So Magritte foresees
the moment when "the object of poetry would become a
knowledge of the secrets of the universe that permits us to
act upon the elements." In this way the role of art becomes
magical. Through art "magical operations would become
possible," writes Magritte: "They will satisfy to the full the
profoundly human desire for the marvellous." [24]

The marvellous objects Magritte paints, so often in awe-
some isolation, exemplify a point of view he has expressed in
the final number of *VVV* (1944): "The principal value of
Surrealism seems to me to be that it has reintroduced the
marvellous into everyday possibilities. It has taught that if
reality seemed baleful and flat it is because man did not
know how to see, his glance was limited by an education
deliberately intended to blind him and by an aesthetic censor
inherited from past ages." And so we find in Magritte's
painting an attempt to initiate a re-education designed, as
Aragon put it in *Le Paysan de Paris*, to "plunge us into
mystery."

"Our cities are thus peopled with misunderstood
sphinxes," writes Aragon, "that do not halt the passing
dreamer if he does not turn his meditative distraction in
their direction, that do not pose him any deadly questions."
If, yielding to the attractions of that form of distraction in
which the Surrealist places his trust, man does respond to
the sphinxes of which *Le Paysan de Paris* speaks, then,
Surrealism teaches, "it is once more abysses within himself
that, thanks to these faceless monsters, he will be examining."

If the Surrealist's thought revolves about the same constant preoccupations, this is because these are the problems
he believes it necessary to solve before further advance is
possible to more satisfying revelations. Man's paramount

concern must be to throw off the weight society has laid upon him. Hence Aragon's insistence, in the catalogue *La Peinture au Défi* (1930), that in Surrealism the marvellous represents not merely the negation of reality but the refusal of one form of reality, and consequently "the development of a new relationship, a new reality that this refusal has liberated."

What stimulates Surrealist resistance to the generally accepted view of reality as rigid and fixed is the conviction that only habit gives it stability, and the assurance that habit cannot survive the explosive force of desire. To the Surrealist, as Breton states in *Les Vases communicants,* "everything that objectively *is* is comprised of an ever-widening circle of possibility!" So the Surrealists are adamantly opposed to the acceptance of the confined limits placed upon reality, intent upon exploring the widening circle of possibility which promises to return man to dominance in the world. Therefore the Surrealists deny the conventional utility of the so-called real, seeing in habit and convention enemies to be combatted whenever they are encountered. "Cut the trees if you like, break the stones also," advise Breton and Eluard in *L'Immaculée Conception,* "but beware, beware the livid light of the useful."

The attitude of the Surrealists on this point is reflected in those objects they have presented not as artifact, but as the concrete expression of the wish to depreciate the value of conventional things. These objects have been designed, as the catalogue of the International Surrealist Exhibition of 1938 made clear, to *"lift the interdiction* resulting from the crushing duplication of those which daily fall under our senses and which urge us to consider anything that *might be* outside of themselves as illusory." The Surrealists objects in question are practical proof of the belief, expressed in Breton's introduction to Ernst's *La Femme 100 Têtes* (1929), that "all things are called upon for other uses than those generally attributed to them."

Duchamp had pointed the way when he nailed a coat-hanger to the floor in his home. By this simple gesture he

separated it from its utilitarian associations, in such a way
as to show it as an object existing in its own right. Mabille
was to make explicit the lesson Surrealism learned from
Duchamp in this matter: In the eleventh number of
Minotaure he wrote, "It is a matter of urgency to proclaim
that Mystery and the Marvellous are not outside but inside
things and people, both being transformed every instant,
united as they are by continuous bonds."

The Surrealists have devoted considerable thought to devising and promoting methods suited to making the public
see the marvellous in relation to their mission of discrediting the real and uncovering the surreal. In this connection a
remark of Breton's in the *Second Manifesto of Surrealism* is
particularly worthy of note: "It seems, especially at the
present time, that we may expect much from certain methods of pure deception, the application of which in art and life
would have for effect to fix attention no longer on the real,
or the imaginary, but, how shall I put it, upon the *reverse of
the real.*" Wishing to draw attention to the marvellous,
which is for the Surrealist the reverse of the real, Surrealism—tacitly admitting once more its debt to Duchamp—has
promulgated deception as a fruitful means of provoking its
public to new critical awareness. Surrealism wishes us to see
that things are not necessarily what they seem; nor are they
so easily classified as habit would have us believe. Deception—as in Duchamp's *Why Not Sneeze* (a bird cage containing lumps of marble cut to resemble sugar cubes)—
proves utilitarian associations to be quite unreliable. It in-
culcates wariness and reveals a range of possibilities hidden
in forms that habit prevents us from noticing any longer.
The joke in Surrealist deception has that quality of disrup-
tive humor in which the Surrealists place confidence. It calls
in question our sense of what *is* and what *is not*, by prompting an awareness of what *may be.*

The Surrealists have come to realize how much is lost in
the unquestioning acceptance of the real; and they appreciate how much the real may be transformed by man's approach to it. When no longer submissive to the dictates of the

established order, man may find a new freedom through the
fuller expression of desire, which reveals itself capable of
dominating the world. So, Noël Arnaud, writing in *Trans-
fusion du Verbe*, invites his readers, in the name of Surrealism, to make of things "intercessors between the in-
expressible and us." And the Surrealists have offered us
encouragement in the form of objects embodying their own
sense of the marvellous.

Surrealism's treatment of objects may take essentially
two forms. The first, following the example of Duchamp's
Bicycle Wheel and *Bottle Rack*, are objects chosen from an
inner impulse, an instinctive sympathy that almost invariably precedes comprehension of the attraction exerted by
the object in question. Objects in this category are most
frequently of the fetishistic variety, like those favored by
Dali, who has discussed their significance at considerable
length. The spoon and mask mentioned by Breton in
L'Amour Fou belong among these. Such objects, of course,
owe their significance largely to the chance circumstance of
their discovery, the aptness they seem to have to a given
need in the individual.

The second form of Surrealist object is that in which the
artist has added to chance his own contribution, through
some material modification dictated, one need not say, by
that same inner compulsion that stimulated interest and
confirmed the beneficence of chance. It is important therefore to appreciate that modifications of this kind are acknowledged and given the greatest importance by the Surrealists themselves. The first number of *La Révolution
surréaliste* (1924) carried the noteworthy announcement:
"Any discovery changing the nature, the destination of an
object or of a phenomenon constitutes a Surrealist fact."
Here is more than iconoclasm, the destruction of established
classifications to which things may be consigned without
question or hesitation. Something more is involved, as all
must agree who have looked at Man Ray's *Cadeau* or Meret
Oppenheim's *Le Déjeuner en Fourrure*.

These are Surrealist objects as Dali has defined them in

his *Secret Life:* "absolutely useless from the practical and rational point of view." Yet both are at least reminiscent of things we use every day, without thinking to accord them special attention. Man Ray's *Cadeau* recalls a flat iron, and Oppenheim's *Le Déjeuner en Fourrure* assembles a cup, saucer and spoon. But we can have none of our habitual assurance in handling or contemplating these things. For the flat iron has a line of short nails protruding from its smooth undersurface, while the cup, saucer and spoon are covered with fur. *Cadeau* cannot serve to press clothes nor can the *Dejeuner en Fourrure* be used for drinking.

Examination of objects of which these are representative examples permits an understanding of what Surrealism hopes to obtain by its repudiation of the utilitarian, and by the modification it leaves the artist free to make, in taking his object out of the livid light of the useful. With equal success Man Ray and Meret Oppenheim have contrived to render the object of their choice quite useless for the purpose for which it was originally designed—whether or not they have done so "for the purpose of materializing in a fetishistic way, with the maximum of tangible reality an idea or a fantasy having a delirious character," as Dali would have us believe the creators of Surrealist objects work. They have done so by a kind of joke, specifically Surrealist in character, reflecting the form of humor Breton's *Anthologie de l'Humour noir* calls "a higher revolt of the mind." This is not mere irreverence, but a revolutionary process taking its origin in desire that is no less potent in its effects for being perhaps unconscious. In Surrealism, laughter is anarchic, calling for a revision of standards in every sphere it touches, and appealing directly to a sense of the marvellous. Surrealist laughter is militant, working towards the destruction of the present and the fuller revelation of the future which is the surreal.

So, though it may not be possible to express rationally what has been accomplished in *Cadeau, Le Déjeuner en Fourrure* and objects like them, the artist's interference with the real in favor of what is as yet unreal indicates more than an invitation to the public to look again at what is familiar. Such deliberate intervention rehabilitates form at the expense of utility. The sense of surprise provoked in the spectator is accompanied by a shock sufficient to give him the impression of seeing virtually new objects, closely enough related to those he is accustomed to find to hand, yet quite definitely removed from the classifications recognized by the conscious mind. Thanks to the artists' interference, these objects escape the routine ritual of existence and hint at the presence of the marvellous implicit in the world. The marvellous, we learn, can be revealed—not invented—once we are able to free our minds from the associations operating when we usually look about us. In this way Surrealist marvellous objects fulfil their role of invitation and stimulant to the imagination. They find their value in the coincidence of chance and the marvellous, and typify the Surrealist's trust in the marvellous as a weapon for breaking down barriers, a means of penetrating behind the façade of reality to a world where desire is the only law-giver.

Surrealism's attitude towards the marvellous is now more accurately assessable. The Surrealists have set out to attain that state of mind in which the marvellous—which, from the outset, they consider to be contained in the real—will have become the normal. This state will be achieved not when the marvellous has lost its efficacy or its novelty, but when the world about us will have ceased to possess the power to impose restrictive and depressing limitations upon our imagination. The marvellous represents for the Surrealist an ideal that will not always evade his grasp.

Thus the Surrealist marvellous object is, no less than a Surrealist poem or painting, the outward expression of a spirit always searching, seeking to probe surface reality and bring to light its potentialities, and finding inspiration in revelations that come most often from forms of experience society refuses to recognize as significant for everyday living. If it admits of ridicule and misrepresentation, its prime value is to prompt reflection and warn man to beware of the habitual and the conventional, and to show that Surrealism wishes us to take note of the marvellous here and now.

Here is the reason for the care with which results of a special enquiry, held within the Surrealist group on March 1935, were reported in the sixth number of *Le Surréalisme au service de la Révolution.* Published under the title "Recherches expérimentales sur certaines possibilité d'Embellissement irrationnel d'une Ville," this *enquête* placed on record replies submitted by a number of Surrealists who had been asked whether certain well-known Paris landmarks should be retained, moved to another place, modified, transformed or destroyed. The replies set down were, we are assured, spontaneous, and therefore closely akin to those statements that find expression in automatic writing, and other practices in which reflection is ruled out. Conducted, Eluard tells us, "with the maximum seriousness," though without preconceived ideas, the enquiry testifies to Surrealism's determination to work out its problems face to face with reality rather than in turning away from it.

Sometimes the answers noted by Eluard are brutally short, reflecting—and occasionally obscenely—Surrealism's arrogant iconoclasm. Other replies, though less impatiently brief, epitomize the Surrealists' refusal to abide by judgements that have led to a form of veneration which is no more than the consecration tradition accords. Even here, then, is to be detected a deliberately irreverent note, with an undertone of seriousness concealed frequently behind the brand of humor in which Surrealism specializes.

This enquiry offers proof of the Surrealists' aspiration to a state of perception and experience that will permit them to witness the complete transformation of the world of concrete reality in response to man's desire, alone considered capable of bringing the marvellous within reach. Here the Surrealist effort to act upon reality is expressively voiced. Absurdity, incongruity, *distraction,* and all other forms of opposition marshalled by Surrealism in its struggle against blind acceptance and static conventions, constitute an attack upon the unyielding façade of a world that will not recognize its own limitations, and which is thus incapable of ensuring the happiness of mankind.

Whether the Surrealist talks of making the final leap, or of crossing the bridge, or of penetrating to the other side of the mirror, his ambitions remain the same, as does his confidence that they will be fulfilled only with the help of imagination. Surrealism declares imagination to be possessed of limitless power to give man the opportunity to bend the world to his desire, to modify it according to the demands he feels entitled to make of it. Reflecting upon his dreams, weighing the discoveries he owes to the practice of automatism and to the revelations of chance, responsive to the sense of liberation made possible by prospecting the world of the irrational, the Surrealist can draw only one conclusion: the marvellous—which is no more than the projection of the surreal he hopes one day to experience fully— is not that which might have been. It is, in fact, that which may be, and must be. The marvellous is what man can make it, by submission to no authority but that of his own desire.

THE GRAND BATTUE OF DESIRE 9

Love, poetry, art, it is thanks to their stimulus that confidence will return, that human thought will succeed in putting to sea once more. André Breton

Breton has remarked in *Entretiens* that it is too often forgotten that Surrealism is much given to *love,* and that "what it stigmatizes passionately is exactly that which may damage the cause of love." Consideration of Surrealism' attitude towards love has been postponed until now, in this examination of Surrealist ambitions, because a discussion of this question conveniently provides the occasion to summarize the main tendencies in Surrealist thought, as these have found expression in art and literature.

The Surrealists' treatment of love provides a point of focus for activities sometimes apparently so diverse as to seem unrelated to one another. But this does not mean that Surrealist behavior before love is without complexity. On the contrary, love may inspire in the Surrealist a variety of sensations at once, and the creative energy it liberates may appeal at the same time to several levels of experience.

However one fact is indisputable: whatever else it may be shown to be, Surrealism's attitude towards love represents a public declaration of faith in the primacy of desire, and for this reason merits special attention.

The importance accorded in Surrealism to dream experience, the recurrent practice of automatism, the cult of chance, as well as the eager exploration of the irrational and the marvellous, all presuppose the same motivating impulse. All may be traced to the generative source of desire, which the Surrealists see as beneficently guiding man along the path of greater knowledge, both of himself and of the world about him. An awareness of the importance Surrealism attaches to desire and of the role it plays in crystallizing Surrealist thought is needed to render evident the fundamental coherence of a whole system of ideas and range of technical devices that might otherwise appear only tenuously interrelated. In spite of certain fluctuations of emphasis, the essential point remains clear: the Surrealists view poetic and artistic productivity as the result of a double stimulus—erotic and psychological, acknowledged by Breton in the "Dreams" number of *Cahiers GLM:* "that which is a function of desire and a function of understanding." The seminal value of desire is recognized in the name of the Surrealists by Judith Reigl: "The essential basis of all creative activity is the despairing desire to destroy the contradictions and the limits of personal existence, both human and universal, to grow in extent thanks to a permanent revolt." [1] But the very fact that Surrealist desire is revolutionary is sufficient to dispose of the suggestion that it could be entirely pessimistic in trend. Desire, as the Surrealists feel it necessary to follow its directives, stands for a categorical refusal to accept the present, and the need to surpass it, to rise above and beyond the boundaries of the real. For the Surrealists have set out to discover and implement a myth suited to life in our times. They never lose from sight the fact that the vitality of this myth is related to the fulfilment of desire. As Breton wrote when introducing the International Surrealist Exhibition of 1947, the new myth await-

ing us stands at the convergence of "the scattered frag-
mentary forms of collective desire."

Desire would be meaningless in Surrealism if it were
synonymous with frustrated needs and sterile yearning. So
what is important is what Simon Watson Taylor has been
able to affirm in *Free Unions:* "In Surrealist poetry, the
expression of desire is synonymous with its fulfilment, for
the act of imagining is in itself the act of realization: *the
power of desire becomes absolute.*" To the Surrealist, desire
is at once awaiting, expectation, and realization. So Surrealist painting, like poetry, remains, in Breton's phrase,
"potentially able to re-create itself ceaselessly so as to trans-
late in its continued fluctuations human desire." Thus the
Surrealist perpetually celebrates what Gascoyne's poem
"Charity Week" calls "the great bursting womb of desire,"
in which modification of the real may truly be offered as a
form of *correction.* In all the forms through which it has
found means of projecting itself into the real world, Surrealism favors the moment of which Breton writes in his
Ode à Charles Fourier:

Quand s'organise la grande battue nocturne du désir
Dans une forêt dont tous les oiseaux sont de flammes.

As nothing in common experience so directly reflects the
power of desire as does love, there is every reason to expect
the Surrealists to attribute to the love instinct special power,
and to invest the sexual act with particular meaning.

However the latter is considered relevant only within
certain clearly defined limits. In *Arcane 17,* where Breton
significantly refers to love as a state of grace, is to be found
the important statement: "The act of love, just like the
picture or the poem, is disqualified if, on the part of the
person giving himself to it, it does not presuppose *entering
into a trance.*" The state of trance, so well suited to precipitating dream experience, favoring automatic revelations
and hallucinatory encounters with the irrational and the
marvellous, is that most favorable to the full realization

guaranteed by love. And it must not be forgotten that, "from a certain point of view the efforts constantly made to reduce antimonies, the Surrealist preoccupations in whatever domain one chooses to consider, converge towards the passionate exaltation of love." [2] Thus love raises questions of direct relevance to the basic problems the Surrealists hope to solve. In their approach to love, they show themselves as much concerned as elsewhere to find solutions they regard as essential.

Already by the end of the twenties—and Breton has stressed this in *Entretiens*—the two dominant preoccupations of Surrealism had become clarified as revolutionary action and love. And these two concerns were, and still are, interrelated. Indeed the Surrealists' defence of the unhindered expression of the love interest—evidenced in their support for Charlie Chaplin when his marital conduct was under criticism,[3] as much as in their "Enquête sur la Sexualité" [4] may readily be interpreted as an exemplifying their characteristic inconoclasm and resistance to convention. But there is more involved than this.

Surrealism rejects the Christian myth in favor of a myth of its own choosing, in the conviction that only as divine love gives way to human love will restraints cease to curb the full expression of desire, to which mankind will finally owe self-knowledge—the prerequisite for a fuller comprehension of human destiny. Iconoclasm is indeed needed. But it must be given direction and purpose. The love instinct must lead somewhere; the erotic must have its point.

One could hardly hope for better guidance on this matter than has been given by Breton. Writing a "Hommage to Max Walter Svanberg," [5] Breton has noted, "Svanberg, it must be said, does us the honors of a world that is none other than that of the 'scabrous,' in the most subversive sense of the word." This fact emphasized, Breton continues with the significant confession, "I have always thought, for my own part, that a certain scabrous element, circumscribed on the erotic plane, by which we are enraptured in certain dreams to the point of retaining for them the most cruel nostalgia, is all that has been able to give man an idea of paradise." Here is the line of thought that leads Breton to consider love as a state of grace. And it is this, too, that places, in Surrealism, definite limits upon eroticism.

This is not to say that Breton's words authorize the dismissal of quite a considerable amount of material, for which the Surrealists have been responsible, in which the erotic is flaunted before a scandalized public. Titles of literary Surrealist works like Léo Malet's *Ne pas Voir plus loin que le Bout de son Sexe,* Aragon's *Le Con d'Irène* and Péret's *Les Couilles enragées* are indication enough to the lengths to which the Surrealists are prepared to go in recording their nonconformism and in offending society. But such extreme cases do nothing to invalidate Surrealism's use of eroticism as a weapon in the struggle for the attainment of the surreal. The very nature of eroticism ensures its adaptability to Surrealism's needs.

In *Le Paysan de Paris* Aragon calls eroticism "an outlaw principle, an irrepressible sense of violation, contempt for prohibition, and taste for confusion." And another former Surrealist, Georges Bataille has offered this definition of the erotic principle in his *L'Erotisme* (1957) : "We speak of eroticism every time a human being conducts himself in a manner that presents a contrasting oppositon of habitual conduction and judgements. Eroticism gives us a glimpse of the *reverse* of a façade whose appearance is never denied: on the *reverse* are revealed feelings, parts of the body and ways of existence of which we are generally ashamed." Thus the revelance of eroticism to the mission of the Surrealists is made plain. Surrealism, wishing to reveal the reverse of habitual reality, finds eroticism in sympathy with its aims.

It is, then, no accident, that the Surrealists stand in the forefront of those who, in our century, have worked for the rehabilitation of the Marquis de Sade. In his first manifesto, Breton speaks of Sade as "Surrealist in sadism," and insists that Sade's desire for moral and social affranchisement is beyond question. Desnos has claimed in his *De L'Erotisme* (1952) that "all our present aspirations were basically formulated by Sade." Meanwhile two of Sade's most serious students—Maurice Heine and Gilbert Lely—have been associated with the Surrealist group. For Sade's influence upon Surrealism goes deeper than its indisputable revolutionary quality would prepare us to expect. It is possible to see in the Surrealists the modern counterparts of the heroes presented in Sade's novels, as Robert Desnos has characterized them in *De L'Erotisme:* "haunted by the desire to bring into accord their exterior existence and their interior lives." Small wonder that the Seventh International Surrealist Exhibition in Paris in 1960 was placed under the aegis of D. A. F. Sade.

"From the erotic point of view," Desnos explains, "the work of Sade is intellectual to a very high degree. . . . It is the creation of an absolutely new universe." In their search for a new universe of their own, the Surrealists have wished to follow the example of the author of *Juliette,* released as they find themselves by Sade's indifference to all demands except those of desire. There is, indeed, in Sade, a fundamental feeling of frustration, that liberates the desire to go even further than the author's frenzied imagination will take him. This desire for freedom, for possession of something at present denied man, is quite clear in the ambitions Surrealism has helped to clarify and give prominence.

Luis Bunuel's film *L'Age d'Or* (1930)—in which the final scene is directly inspired by Sade's *Les Vingt-Cinq Journées de Sodome*—is but one instance of Sade's influence upon Surrealist activity. Tributes, both verbal and pictorial,[6] have been repeatedly paid to Sade by the defenders of Surrealism, but nowhere more directly than in the paintings of Clovis Trouille and Wilhelm Freddie—the latter the only Surrealist to have the distinction of seeing some of his pictures hanging in the Copenhagen Criminological Museum.

Response to the literary production of Joyce Mansour has been less dramatic, it is true, but her work is no less scandalous. Eroticism is the connecting thread running through her prose works—*Jules César* (1954) and *Les Gisants satis-*

faits (1958)—and her poetry—*Cris* (1953), *Déchirures* (1955) and *Rapaces* (1960).

The main inspiration in Mansour's work is unmistakably sadistic. So much so that the most apt parallel for her poetry seems to be "those images of convulsive eroticism," as Nora Mitrani has called Hans Bellmer's photographs of his doll with detachable legs, arms and head. Bellmer has written in his *Vingt-Cinq Reproductions* (1950) that the human body is comparable to a sentence which we may take to pieces so as to use its elements to compose a series of anagrams that constitute "its true content." An analogous process of thought might have resulted in the lines of Joyce Mansour beginning in "Noyée au fond d'un rêve ennuyeux." In fact, Mitrani might have had Mansour in mind also, when she remarked, in an article reprinted in *Vingt-Cinq Reproductions*, that all Bellmer's research is directed toward elucidating, perfecting and extending "that mode of correspondence, the physiological with the psychic, and the psychic with the objective": Mansour, in *Déchirures*, begins a poem with "Invitez-moi à passer la nuit dans votre bouche."

So, in the poetry of Joyce Mansour may be detected more than a note of protest against conventionality. Eroticism is allied to another characteristic that now calls for consideration if a balanced impression is to be obtained of the role Surrealism reserves for love in literature, art and life.

At the end of 1929 the twelfth number of *La Révolution surréaliste* carried a questionnaire on love. Referring to this, Breton assures the readers of *Entretiens* (1952) that the enquiry opened by that questionnaire is still not closed: the questions posed in 1929 remain of supreme importance for the Surrealists. They are therefore worth quoting, at least in part: "What sort of hope do you place in love? How do you imagine the movement from the *idea of love* to the *fact of love?* Would you willingly or otherwise sacrifice to love your liberty? Have you done so? . . . Do you believe in the victory of love over sordid life or of sordid life over admirable love?" These questions, more or less explicitly phrased, recur throughout the last forty years of Surrealist effort. What is more, in condensed form they reappear in the fifth number of *BIEF*, in March 1959: "What does 'love at first sight' represent for you, and what changes might it bring in your life?" The phrasing of the crucial question is significant in indicating Surrealism's continuing adherence to the principle that abstract contemplation is no more valid than escapist literature: love, like art and poetry, must been seen to act upon life. In the circumstances, therefore, it is interesting to note the reply of the poet Guy Cabanel, recorded in the seventh issue of the same review. For Cabanel, love at first sight represents the very transformation of life, "for things are no longer seen from the same angle, but in their hidden aspect, which implies a communion between man and the universe."

Cabanel's reply that so aptly sums up the feelings expressed in his *Maliduse* (1961) are a valuable reminder that Surrealism does not wish to dissociate man and the universe, but to reunite them in a new understanding, to be brought about by a number of means, of which not the least is love.

To the Surrealist, the face of a beautiful woman, as Breton and Eluard wrote in *L'Immaculée Conception*, is "the pearl worth a thousand times over the death of the diver." Its presence and enigma haunts the photographs of Man Ray and the canvases of Paul Delvaux. For both these artists, viewing the world as Surrealists, have sensed that woman holds the key to man's destiny, and that she is to be approached, consequently, in a mood of anguished expectancy. Woman, in Surrealism is, in fact, the very projection of the marvellous into our dreary existence; love for woman what Breton's poem *Fata Morgana* calls "that promise which goes beyond us." Through love man may hope for paradise regained. Through woman he may dream of regeneration.

In considerable measures woman, the personification of desire, is the revelation of chance. Which is why Breton, as a young man, would leave open his bedroom door at night, looking to the chance encounter he hoped to make possible by this gesture for a new direction to his life. His poem "Et Mouvement encore" in *L'Air et l'Eau* (1934) celebrates such a meeting:

> Cette rencontre
> Avec tout ce qu'elle comporte à distance de fatal
> Cette précipitation l'un vers l'autre de deux systèmes
>   tenus séparément pour subjectifs
> Met en branle une série de phénomènes très réels
> Qui concourent à la formation d'un monde distinct
> De nature à faire honte de ce que nous apercevrions
> A son défaut.[7]

And in the verses beginning "On me dit que là-bas les plages sont noires," Breton asks:

> Quel est donc ce pays lointain
> Qui semble tirer toute sa lumière de ta vie
> Il tremble bien réel à la pointe de tes cils.[8]

Breton shows that, if the discovery of this country can be his, it is only through the intervention of woman. Thus *Arcane 17* (1944) speaks of "the revelation you brought me," and adds "before even knowing what it might consist in, I knew it was a revelation." For the Surrealist, the exact nature of the revelation mankind owes to woman is less important than the recognition that he may find in her a mediatrix, making communication with the surreal possible.

Here is one of the major myths of Surrealism, examined with care in Péret's *Anthologie de l'Amour sublime* (1956), a myth that entitles Trost to speak of "the poetic initiation of love." In his *Visible et Invisible* (1953), Trost remarks, "And more than ever it rests with *woman* to make it possible for us to find that conciliation of the visible world with the invisible world," which Breton's *Arcane 17* calls "the fusion of existence and essence." Thanks to love, the Surrealist proclaims, complete harmony will be established: "the great malediction is raised."

Hence Surrealism repeatedly pays its respects to what *Les Vases communicants* terms "the exceptional grandeur and value of human love." Breton's "mad love" of *L'Amour fou* (1937) is the "sublime love" of Péret's anthology. "And when I speak of love," Gui Rosey remarks pertinently, "I evoke especially that instant when sensual pleasure consummates the union of dream and action." [9] The sense of expansion, of affranchisement made possible by love therefore becomes the recurrent theme of Eluard's Surrealist poetry:

Et toujours un seul couple uni par un seul vêtement
Par le même désir
Couché aux pieds de son reflet
Un couple illimité.[10]

In Surrealism the role of woman is to give man the opportunity to resist and react against what *Arcane 17* calls *opacity*—"the greatest enemy of man." Hence the imagery used, for instance, by René Crevel: "To the all too classic fable of Psyche losing love for having wished to know it, is opposed the reality of the creature who is loved. A face, *a face that pierces walls*, is revealed and triumphs *to the detriment of silence*." [11] The marvellous revelation made possible by contact with woman may, perhaps, be of brief duration. But as the Breton poem commencing "Au beau demi-jour de 1934" (*L'Air de l'Eau*) shows, there is still cause for hope. The poet will record his gratitude and veneration, communicating his adoration for a being who can occasion such a feeling of release from mundane limitations. Here, then, is the source of the strange images to be found in Péret's love poems; "Allo," for instance, from *Je Sublime* (1936):

Mon avion en flammes mon château inondé de vin du
    Rhin
mon ghetto d'iris noirs mon oreille de cristal

mon rocher dévalant la falaise pour écraser la garde champêtre.[12]

Whether evoked through the "convulsive" images of Péret, or the deceptively simple verse of Mesens and Eluard, woman remains the same for the Surrealist poet: "No one could say with certainty if she is beautiful but everyone has seen her beautify the places through which she passes, everyone has seen her capture the suburbs in distress with the pearly lasso of her breath." [13] The ability, if not to transform the world, then to make man see it transformed is the source of the mystery of woman for the Surrealists. As in Mesens' verses "Je ferme les yeux," woman evades his efforts to comprehend her mystery. But this in no way impairs her capacity to offer inspiration, as Mesens' "Ce Soir" bears witness:

La pointe de tes yeux
Sur la pointe de tes seins
Tes yeux dans mon sein
Et tes seins dans ma tête
A l'heure où rien dans le miroir ne guette
Je pars sur un long chemin où plus rien ne m'arrête.[14]

And so the Surrealist poet will be less inclined to sing his passion for woman than the discoveries his passion has enabled him to make:

Des vols de perroquets traversent ma tête quand je te vois
  de profil
et le ciel de graisse se strie d'éclairs bleus
qui tracent ton nom dans tous les sens.[15]

The unquestioning faith in woman's capacity to ensure access to the world of the surreal endows Surrealist love poetry—whether it be tender, passionate or violent—with an optimism that no one has put into words better than Eluard:

Les chemins tendres que trace ton sang clair
Joignent les créatures
C'est de la mousse qui recouvre le désert
Sans que la nuit jamais puisse y laisser
    d'empreintes ni d'ornières.[16]

For the Surrealist the presence of woman in the world is proof that man's redemption is within his grasp, and requires no outside agency to make it effective. Woman is capable of giving life meaning, of elevating it to significance, because she possesses the power to mediate between man and the marvellous. Surrealism's confidence in love is thus indicative of optimism regarding man's future in a universe at present seemingly oppressive in its influence. Love and woman are, in Surrealism, symbolic not simply of rejection, iconoclasm and the assertion of personal liberty in the face of social restraint, but also of the essential principles upon which the Surrealists have sought to build. Love proves that, to the Surrealist, evasion is less valuable than transformation. It stands for action, not withdrawal; for change in the world, not for immobility or the unresisting acceptance of an unhappy fate. Love transmutes vision, submitting the world to its own demands, while rejecting all that, in our present life, stands between us and the fulfillment of desire. Love therefore calls upon man to face life, and to see in the repudiation of constraint a new liberty, not a reluctance to assume responsibility. Thanks to love, man glimpses the kind of experience that can be his when, objective chance and the other means called to his aid having taken their effect, the marvellous ceases to be marvellous and becomes natural. This is the moment of the full attainment of desire; the moment when aspirations coincide with realizations.

The process of refinement demanded of the individual by love is but the first step. It permits him to grasp the thread of which Breton writes in his poem "Vigilance," the thread he will refuse to surrender until it has led him, through the mirror of banal relationships and appearances, to another form of perception and cognizance, into the world of the surreal. Sustained in the journey he has undertaken by the illuminating presence of woman, man finds that the surreal —when correctly viewed—is the real: that form of reality from which so much in life seems to separate him and which, if it were not for desire, might have forever eluded him.

Soon will come equilibrists in jerkins span-
gled with an unknown colour, the only colour
that today absorbs the rays of the sun and
moon. This colour will be called freedom and
the sky will flap all its blue and black pen-
nants, because for the first time a wind fully
propitious will rise, and those who are there
will understand that they have set sail, and
that all preceding pretended voyages were
only a decoy.   André Breton

If one fact finds repeated stress in the Surrealists' writings
on literature and painting, it is that these are to be regarded
as means, and not as ends in themselves. We encounter the
same lack of concern for Art with a capital letter which
Dada had taught, whether it is the attitude of the Surrealist
painter or of the poet that comes under discussion. Surrealism has never aimed at the enrichment of a given artistic
form, and if it has been prompt to take advantages of the
opportunities offered by art and literature, Surrealism has
not deviated from its primary, extra-literary and extra-
artistic aims.

The state of mind in which the Surrealist approaches his task is illuminated by Marcel Mariën, who wrote in his *La Chaise de Sable* (1940) that, to the painter for example, painting is "pure coincidence, pure means." And this "means" must not preoccupy the Surrealist beyond its relevance to his purpose. Numerous testimonials of the same kind prove the existence, for the Surrealist, of something that takes precedence over mere technical mastery. They indicate beyond doubt that, in Surrealism, interest in technique can be only incidental. No genuine Surrealist would depart from the view that the art he practices is an instrument to be put to special use.

In some measure, of course, the use reserved for art by the Surrealist is a private one, dictated by the individual's wish to discover and explore for himself what the surreal contains. Thus in the drawings of Robert Lagarde, for instance, "the discomfort," as Alain Joubert has emphasized,[1] "comes from *inside*." However, it would be incorrect to consider Surrealist art as entirely selfish, indifferent to the outsider, and appealing only to those perfectly attuned to the artist's feelings. Thanks to the collective unconscious to which the Surrealist appeals with the fullest confidence, the experience of the artist, though finding its source at depths unrecognized by the conscious mind, becomes that of the spectator or reader. The Surrealist's attitude on this matter permits of no equivocation: "The function of the different elements brought into play by the painter-poet," writes Masson, "will take place with the flashing rapidity of light. The unconscious and the conscious, intuition and understanding must operate their transmutation in the subconscious mind in radiant unity."[2]

The Surrealist's discovery of a model within himself—in a process that accompanies his search for true identity—and the manner in which he renders his impressions entail in his public a reaction involving more than their sensibility alone. Masson speaks of transmutation, and Péret, à propos the painting of Wifredo Lam, writes: "The true mission of the

artist—painter or poet—has always consisted in discovering in himself the archetypes underlying poetic thought, to
charge them with new affectivity, so that a current of energy
circulates between his fellow-men and himself, all the more
intensely because these archetypes, once actualized, will appear as the renewed and heightened expression of the en-
vironment that has conditioned the artist." [3] Péret, it is to be
noticed, identifies poetry with painting and demands of both
the same contribution to progress towards the surreal. And
so Sarane Alexandrian's remark on the relation of the Surrealist poet to his public applies equally well to the Surrealist painter and his: "The relation between the poet and
his public is strictly that of initiator and initiated, with all
the mysterious complicity and all the uplift this presupposes
on both sides." [4] But what sort of initiation?

In the eleventh number of *Minotaure*, Jean Cazaux distinguished two attitudes between which, he declared, the Surrealist poet, oscillates: docility and revolt. The poet's
docility—so perfectly evidenced in the practice of automatic
techniques and methods that invite the aid of chance—
presupposes, according to Cazaux, revolt as its point of
departure, just as it finds in revolt a spur and a support. In
this way Cazaux sees docility and revolt as interpenetrating
to the point where it is difficult to distinguish, at any given
moment, the contribution each is making. But we need not
doubt that, in the final analysis, this is of no consequence.
What matters is that poetry—understood in the widest sense
Surrealism authorizes—is conceived by the Surrealists as "a
means of getting out, a tool ideally suited to breaking certain
limits." [5] For this reason, interest in aesthetic problems that
command the attention of so many artists always takes
second place in Surrealism to considerations of how best to
produce that "mental electricity" for which, according to
Breton's *Arcane 17*, poetry is the conductor. Any valid estimation of the means Surrealism uses must result from a

clear identification of the mental electricity these means are designed to produce.

In the fourth number of the review *Médium,* Paalen exalts "the joy of the virgin glance," and, in the name of the Surrealist painters, proposes to discover "the potential prolongation of things" through affective knowledge, which he terms "infra and ultra-forms." Here may be detected the deep motive force of Surrealism in an instinct for total liberation. Such liberation requires social and political freedom, but implies enfranchisement on a much wider plane also. Following the lead of the sociologist Fourier—who has exerted an increasing influence over Breton's thought—the Surrealists have wished to "revise human understanding." Jean-Louis Bédouin explains, in the third number of *Médium:*

Starting from a refusal of the derisory condition to which man is reduced by constraints of every nature, Surrealism is the passionate search for "the powers of the Spirit," an unprecedented attempt to restitute them to him. The idea that the limits imposed upon all expression can be abolished, thanks to appropriate methods, guides it in the domain of poetry which is specifically though not restrictively its own. In life, in the same way, it is a question of setting in motion the secret mainsprings of being, so as to change this life, which is so to speak conceded to us, into a real life, at last worth living.

Escape from constraint but not evasion of life—this is important to the Surrealist. Escape through a form of action that will effect the transformation of life. But—and Eluard made the point with some emphasis during a lecture in London in 1936, upon the occasion of the International Surrealist Exhibition—escape is compatible with Surrealism only provided it offers salvation to others as well as to the poet: "The time is come when all poets have the right and the duty to maintain that they are deeply involved in the lives of other men, in common life." Thus the limits Surrealism assigns to creative activity in its liberating force are not the narrow framework of the poem or the picture. They are, in Yves Bonnefoy's phrase, "the moving limits of our existence." [6]

Placing man at the centre of the universe, Surrealism lays
upon his shoulders the burden of his own salvation, and says
with Masson:

> Au centre du monde est l'homme
> Il est le point le cercle et le rayon
> Du haut en has sa forme entière
> Par une épée très pure est traversée [7]

Looking back upon his years as a Surrealist, Masson remarked in his *Entretiens avec Georges Charbonnier* that
Surrealism is "the only liberating movement, the only liberating idea there has been in France. In the world . . ."
The Surrealists, indeed, say with Breton's poem "Non-
Lieu," "Never liberty except for liberty." It is therefore
significant that Raymond Queneau, explaining in an interview with Gilbert Ganne what attracted him to Surrealism,
has stated: "It was not from the literary point of view
that Surrealism interested me, but as a mode of life. It
was complete revolt. . . . For me, Surrealism represented
everything." [8] Paalen is more explicit: "In Surrealism alone
I found experience lived to the full, the heroic attempt at an
integral synthesis which admitted no more arbitrary separa-
tion between plastic expression and poetry, between poetry
and life." [9] It is the spirit of Surrealism that is acknowledged in both cases. A spirit that Desnos has called "the
solidarity of those who are going to blow up a town in the
spirit of revolt." [10] Here is the sense of unity that has remained a feature of the Surrealist group and which, paradoxical as it seems, has contributed in no small measure to
precipitating violent quarrels and dramatic exclusions.

Surrealism has remained against "all that is opposed to
the emancipation of the spirit," of which the first indispen-
sable condition, as the opening number of *VVV* (1942)
stresses, is the liberation of man. The prefatory note reproduced in each number of *VVV* therefore speaks of a
synthesis of the external view and the internal—what man
sees outside himself, and what he sees within—aimed at

resolving their contradiction through "a systematic en-
largement of the field of consciousness towards a total
view." This is to say that the Surrealists have in view the
dialectical conciliation of physical perception and mental
representation. If, in Surrealism, the methods of psycho-
analysis are highly regarded it is because, to quote Breton
in *Nadja,* they "expel man from himself." Furthermore, "it
is the universe that must be interrogated first of all about
man and not man about the universe." [11]

What is needed above all is that "acute poetic *availability*"
which Joubert claims as necessary for a comprehension of
the work of Brauner.[12] In the absence of this essential responsiveness, the Surrealist poet cannot function as he
should: as one who inspires, rather than one who is inspired.
For the Surrealists are in agreement with Breton, whose *Le
Surréalisme et la Peinture* speaks of "a particular philoso-
phy of immanence" according to which surreality is contained in reality and is neither superior nor exterior to it.
They have always attempted to present interior reality and
exterior reality as "two elements in process of unification, of
finally becoming one." This final unification, the supreme
aim of Surrealism, can be brought about, they believe, only
by the full understanding of the qualities and capabilities of
the human personality. And this, as Breton told the students
to whom he lectured at Yale University, cannot be effected
without "a general revision of the modes of knowledge,"
that will result in "lifting the malediction of an uncrossed
barrier between the external and the internal world that, if
rediscovered, would be the salvation of man." [13]

This is the motivation behind the whole technical effort of
Surrealism, that has consisted, says Breton, in multiplying
ways of reaching "the most profound levels of the mental
personality." The ambition underlying and promoting this
activity is, no doubt, what most differentiates Surrealism
from Dadaism, and marks a logical step forward, beyond
derision to a newly conceived form of provocation that is, in
itself, a form of invitation. In the third number of *La Révolution surréaliste,* Antonin Artaud spoke of "a certain Sur-

real eternity," towards which Surrealism was already aiming. Echoing these words over more than a quarter of a century of struggle against repression, Breton has emphasized "that education of the understanding which is our aim—to transform the world, to change life." [14]

Taking our point of departure in Breton's words, we may summarize the trends that have characterized active Surrealism since the early twenties. Surrealist practice takes us through two stages of experience. First disturbing our sense of reality, as it discredits the world of everyday convention and habitual relationships, it then reveals and sets about exploring another world, that of the surreal which it has brought within reach. There are serious disadvantages in making even at this point such a clear distinction. One risks suggesting that Surrealism passes through two separate stages. It might be concluded that we must look to the work of one artist to typify the first stage, and to another for the second. The conclusion then would appear to be that the Surrealists approach their task fully aware they must have one of two possible aims in view. This would be saying they are—and must be—quite cerebral in their attitude toward their art, conscious of a logical, and even of a chronological progression toward the surreal, and placing exact limits upon the effect they wish to produce. Nevertheless, the advantages of viewing in this way what Surrealism accomplishes can be appreciated. One is able to discern and identify without misrepresentation a general pattern that, without injustice, permits us to pay tribute to the underlying coherence of Surrealist thought and practice. At the same time one perceives more readily the relevance of many incidental preoccupations that have held the Surrealists' attention over the years: the interest shown in primitive art, the fascination exerted by the myth of the Holy Grail, their attraction to Lewis Carroll as much as to Sade . . . One becomes aware, too, of a movement forward, an instinct which, even if it appears to be working against itself sometimes, is advancing toward something valuable. And one detects meaning where meaning is frequently denied.

Whether the various techniques employed in Surrealism impress as constructive or as destructive, they must be acknowledged as making their necessary contribution to advancing the ultimate aims the Surrealists have never lost from sight and which have given Surrealism an importance this century cannot deny.

The haunting presence of Surrealism is still with us and continues, as Breton's *Entretiens* affirms, to imply "the maximum of *adventure*." So far as Surrealism is concerned, it matters little who has fallen by the wayside, or who has been sacrificed in the persistent advance. Soupault and Artaud were among the first to be expelled for succumbing to the temptation to reduce Surrealism to a literary technique. Aragon fell from favor when he became unable to see that political conformism in whatever form is incompatible with revolutionary Surrealism. Ernst has been excluded for a gesture—the acceptance of the Grand Prix for Painting at the Venice Biennale in 1955—which the Surrealists interpret as compromising his artistic independence. But the essential vitality of Surrealism remains, and owes its survival to the strict demands it makes of its adherents. As leader of the group, Breton stands convinced, as his recent interview in the newspaper *Le Monde* shows, that, if Surrealism is to retain the purity of its aims, to resist the contamination he believes must inevitably follow upon conformism, then "vigilance is the rule." This is because, as one Surrealist has said, "Our world is a world perpetually *becoming*." [15] In his *Position politique du Surréalisme*, Breton, writing of Surrealism, speaks of "constants" and "variables," and stresses the word *function*. Reviewing four decades of Surrealist activity, one may say that what has remained constant is the instinct for total liberation; the variable elements being the technical mechanism that have been delegated the function of effecting the liberation to which the Surrealist aspires.

"Fewer manifestoes, more works!" Marcel Jean, who in his *Histoire de la Peinture Surréaliste* (1959) cites this now familiar criticism of Surrealism, counters: "But has not Surrealism wished to be a preface, repeatedly renewed? In the new poets and painters, real existence is that of the future. What has already been realized, known, acclaimed, that loses the character of pure potentiality to assume a determined, final, fixed aspect, also loses, for them, much of its interest. The past is memory; while the future is based upon the creative faculty." If Jean's words seem an excuse offered rather hastily and at a late date, it is as well to recall that they add little or nothing to what Aragon wrote in a celebrated article, "Une Vague de Rêves:" [16] "You can see then what the surreal is. But grasping a notion of it can only be done by extension; at best it is a notion that slips away like the horizon before the walker, for like the horizon it is a relationship between the spirit and that which it will never attain."

Perhaps, indeed, the ultimate ambitions of the Surrealists are so remote as to defy realization. But hasty conclusions here will do nothing to solve the important question of the true value of Surrealism. As Breton remarked in *Le Monde* in 1962: "You don't assess results when you feel yourself still on the move, and whatever conquests have been obtained, there always remains something more to conquer." The modesty and the arrogance of Surrealism guarantees its survival. Characteristically therefore, the first number of Surrealism's latest review, *La Brèche* (October 1961), opens with the announcement: "We have no power but that of our desires. We have not finished being in the right."

NOTES

PREFACE

1. See J. H. Matthews, "Literary Surrealism in France since 1945," in *Books Abroad,* XXXVI, no. 4 (Autumn 1962), pp. 356–64, and "Some Post-War Surrealist Poets," in *Yale French Studies,* no. 31 (May 1964), pp. 145–53. A comprehensive listing of Surrealist publications will appear in *Comparative Literature Studies.*

2. See, for example, the catalogue of the Toyen exhibition at the Galerie Furstenberg, Paris, in May, 1958. It consists entirely of brief texts by Robert Benayoun, André Breton, Yves Elléouet, Georges Goldfayn, E. L. T. Mesens, Benjamin Péret and Jean-Claude Silbermann.

3. Cited in Charles Estienne and José Pierre, "Situation de la peinture en 1954," in *Médium,* nouvelle série, no. 4 (January 1955), p. 44.

4. *Ibid.*

1 DADA

1. The most complete general studies of Dada are the following: Robert Motherwell, *The Dada Painters and Poets* (New York:

Wittenborn, Schultz, Inc., 1951). Hans Arp, Richard Huelsenbeck, Tristan Tzara, *Dada, Die Geburt es Dada Dichtung und Chronik der Gründer* (Zurich: Peter Schifferil Verlags, 1957). Richard Huelsenbeck, *Mit Witz, Licht und Grütze: Auf den Spuren des Dadaismus* (Wiesbaden: Limes Verlag, 1957). Georges Hugnet, *L'Aventure Dada* (Paris: Galerie de l'Institut, 1957). Willy Verkauf, *Dada: Monograph of a Movement* (London: Alec Tirani, 1957). Georges Ribemont-Dessaignes, *Déjà Jadis ou du Mouvement Dada à l'Espace abstrait* (Paris: Juillard, 1958). Raoul Hausmann, *Courrier Dada* (Paris: Le Terrain Vague, 1958). One may consult also Tristan Tzara, *Sept Manifestes Dada; Lampisteries* (Paris: Jean-Jacques Pauvert, 1963).

2. See Georges Ribemont-Dessaignes, "Histoire de Dada," in *La Nouvelle Revue française*, nos. 213–14 (1931), quoted in Motherwell, *The Dada Painters and Poets*, p. 102.

3. See Herbert S. Gershman, "Futurism and the Origins of Surrealism," in *Italica*, XXXIX, no. 2 (June 1962), 114–23.

4. Quoted Motherwell, *The Dada Painters and Poets*, pp. 28–29.

5. "Some Memories of Pre-Dada: Picabia and Duchamp," in Motherwell, p. 255.

6. See Tzara's "Introduction" to Hugnet's *L'Aventure Dada*, p. 7.

7. Quoted Motherwell, p. xx, from Ball's *Flucht aus der Zeit*, 1927.

8. See Grosz's autobiography, *A Little Yes and a Big No*, trans. Lola Sachs Dorin (New York: The Dial Press, 1948).

2 EMERGENCE OF SURREALISM

1. Breton, *Entretiens 1913–1952* (Paris: Gallimard, 1952), p. 52. This text is particularly valuable for the information it supplies regarding Breton's state of mind at the time when he was attracted to Dada.

2. See J. H. Matthews, "Apollinaire devant les Surréalistes," in 'Guillaume Apollinaire,' 3, *La Revue des Lettres Modernes*, 1964.

3. See Philippe Soupault, "Que reste-t-il de nos amours?" in *Réalités*, no. 160 (November 1959), p. 82.

4. "L'Esprit nouveau et les poètes," in *Mercure de France,* December 1, 1918, p. 394.

5. The question of Surrealism's relations with Communism has been treated by Victor Crastre in his *Le Drame du Surréalisme* (Paris: Les Editions du Temps, 1963).

3 SURREALISM AND THE ARTS

1. *Looking at Modern Painting* (Los Angeles: University of California Department of Art, 1957), p. 66.

2. "A Note on the Exquisite Corpse," in *Yale French Studies,* I, 2 (Fall–Winter 1948), p. 88.

3. "Surrealism cannot be Art," in *Angry Penguins* (Autumn 1944), pp. 53–54.

4. "The Theoretical Background of Surrealism," in *The Journal of Aesthetics and Art Criticism,* II (1948), p. 44.

5. "Magritte un grand surréaliste," in *Arts,* no. 548 (December 28, 1955—January 3, 1956), p. 11.

6. Georges Hugnet, "L'Iconoclaste," in *Cahiers d'Art,* no. 5–6 (1935), p. 220.

7. "In the Light of Surrealism," in Alfred H. Barr Jr., *Fantastic Art, Dada, Surrealism* (New York: The Museum of Modern Art, 3rd edition, 1947), p. 35.

8. "Un surréaliste peut-il être peintre?" in *Arts,* no. 754 (December 23–29, 1959), p. 16.

9. See "Trait d'Union," preface to the catalogue *La Peinture surréaliste en Europe* (Sarrebruck, 1952).

10. "Painting is a Wager" (reprinted from *Cahiers du Sud*) in *Horizon,* VII, no. 39 (March 1943), p. 178.

11. "Cinémage," in *L'Age du Cinéma,* no. 4–5 (August–November, 1951), p. 25.

12. See *The Arts Review,* XIII, no. 17 (September 9–23, 1961), p. 2.

13. *Beyond Painting* (New York: Wittenborn, Schultz, Inc., 1948), p. 7.

14. *Ibid.* p. 8.

15. *Ibid.* p. 9.

16. See Charles Estienne and José Pierre, "Situation de la peinture en 1954," in *Médium*, nouv. série, no. 4 (January 1954), p. 47.

17. "Surrealism, Jackson Pollock, and Lyric-Abstraction," in the catalogue *Surrealist Intrusion in the Enchanters' Domain* (New York: D'Arcy Galleries, 1960), p. 32.

18. See J. H. Matthews, "Poetic Principles of Surrealism," in *Chicago Review*, XV, no. 4 (Summer–Autumn 1962), pp. 27–45; "Surrealism and the Cinema," in *Criticism*, IV, no. 2 (Spring 1962), pp. 120–33; "Du Cinéma comme langage surréaliste," in *Etudes cinématographiques*, Special Number, 'Surréalisme et Cinéma,' forthcoming.

4 A SWING DOOR

1. "Sur la scène du rêve," *Cahiers GLM*, Septième Cahier (March 1938, special "Dreams" number), p. 82.

2. *Man's Life is This Meat* (London: The Parton Press, 1936).

3. This is one of forty-one reasons assembled by Brauner in an article, "Du Fantastique en peinture," in *VVV*, no. 2–3 (March 1945), pp. 74–75.

4. "The Exhibitionist's Overcoat," in *New Road* (Surrealist issue), 1943.

5. "Wolfgang Paalen interroge," in *Médium*, première série, no. 2 (December 1952).

6. Quoted in Sarane Alexandrian, *Victor Brauner, l'Illuminateur* (Paris: Editions Cahiers d'Art, 1954), p. 27.

7. *Towards a New Subject in Painting* (San Francisco: The Museum of Modern Art, 1948), p. 28.

8. "Cinéma et Réalité," in *La Nouvelle Revue française*, November 1927, p. 562.

9. "Notes on the Making of *Un Chien Andalou*," *Art in Cinema*, ed. Frank Stauffacher (San Francisco: The Museum of Modern Art, 1947).

10. "The New Image," in *Dyn*, no. 1 (1942), p. 9.

11. Quoted in James Thrall Soby, *Joan Miró* (New York: The Museum of Modern Art, 1959), p. 7.

12. Pierre Mabille, "Le Miroir," in *Minotaure,* no. 11 (May 1938), p. 68.

13. That which has been understood exists no more
    The bird has become one with the wind
    The sky with its truth
    Man with his reality.

14. *A la grande Nuit ou le Bluff surréaliste* (Paris: chez l'auteur, 1927), reproduced in Artaud's *Œuvres complètes* (Paris: Gallimard, 1956), I, p. 288.

15. See Breton, *Yves Tanguy*—text in French and English with translations by Bravig Imbs (New York: Pierre Matisse, 1946), p. 88. All remarks by Breton on Tanguy cited in this chapter are borrowed from this text, which assembles articles and judgements dating back to Breton's first contact with Tanguy's work.

16. James Thrall Soby, *Yves Tanguy* (New York: The Museum of Modern Art, 1955), p. 17.

17. This, like Gascoyne's other Surrealist verse, is reproduced in *Man's Life is This Meat* (1936).

18. In Paris the unsteady Tour Saint-Jacques
    Like a sunflower
    With its brow comes at times to strike the Seine and its
      shadow glides imperceptibly among the tugboats.

19. At this moment on tip-toe in my sleep
    I make for the room in which I am lying.

20. And I set fire to it
    So that nothing remains of that consent
      extorted from me.

21. The furniture then gives way to animals of the same size
      that look at me fraternally
    Lions in whose manes the chairs are finally consumed
    Dog-fish whose white bellies join with the last
      rustle of sheets
    At the hour of love and blue eyelids.

22. I see myself burn in my turn I see that solemn hiding-place
      of nothings
    That was my body
    Dug into by the patient beaks of ibises of fire.

23. When all is over invisible I enter the ark
    Without a care for the passers-by of life whose
    dragging footsteps resound far off.

24. I see the skeleton of the sun
    Through the hawthorn of the rain
    I hear the human linen tear like
    a great leaf
    Beneath the nail of absence and presence which
    are in connivence
    All trades fade away there remains of them
    only a perfumed lace
    A shell of lace that has the perfect form of a
    breast.

25. I touch no longer but the heart of things I hold the thread.

5 OPEN SESAME

1. "1870–1936," in Herbert Read (ed.), *Surrealism* (London: Faber, 1936), p. 248

2. This may explain the title of Breton's *Poisson soluble* (1924). Born under the sign of Pisces, Breton believes that man is "soluble in his thought."

3. See "L'Iconoclaste," in *Cahiers d'Art*, no. 5–6 (1935), p. 139.

4. "The Exhibitionist's Overcoat," in *New Road* (Surrealist issue), 1943.

5. Introductory note to the English Surrealist review *Free Unions*, 1946.

6. See Noël Arnaud *et al.*, *La Conquête du Monde par l'Image* (Paris: Editions de la Main à Plume, 1942), p. 1.

7. "The New Image," in *Dyn*, no. 1 (1942), p. 8.

8. See A. Breton and J. Schuster, "Art poétique," in *BIEF, Jonction surréaliste*, no. 7 (June 1959).

9. Interview with René Bélance in *Haïti-Journal* (December 12–13, 1945), reproduced in *Entretiens* (Paris: Gallimard 1952), p. 234.

10. "Préface à une Etude sur la Métaphore," in *Le Surréalisme au service de la Révolution*, no. VI (May 1933), p. 27.

11. "Le Message automatique," in *Minotaure*, no. 3–4 (May 1934), p. 62.

12. Christian Dotremont in *La Conquête du Monde par l'Image*, p. 19.

13. "Genèse et Perspective artistique du Surréalisme," cited in Peggy Guggenheim (ed.), *Art of This Century* (New York: Art of This Century, 1942), p. 19.

14. *Ibid.*

15. *Entretiens avec Georges Charbonnier* (Paris: Julliard, 1958), p. 107.

16. Quoted in Gustave Regler, "Four European Painters in Mexico," in *Horizon*, XVI, no. 91 (August 1947), p. 100.

17. "Notes on the Christian Myth," in *Free Unions*, p. 15.

18. See *Surrealist Intrusion in the Enchanters' Domain* (New York: D'Arcy Galleries, 1960), p. 64.

19. See Georges Duthuit, "Où allez-vous Miró?," in *Cahiers d'Art*, no. 8–10 (1936), p. 204.

20. Simon Hantaï and Jean Schuster, "Une Démolition au Platane," in *Médium*, nouv. série, no. 4 (January 1955), p. 61.

21. André Masson, *Entretiens avec Georges Charbonnier*, p. 63.

22. From Breton's poem "Les Attitudes spectrales," in *Le Revolver aux Cheveux blancs* (1932).

6 ORACULAR REPLIES

1. "Comme dans un bois," in *L'Age du Cinéma*, no. 4–5 (August–November 1951), reproduced in his *La Clé des Champs* (Paris: Les Editions du Sagittaire, 1955), p. 242.

2. Yves Bonnefoy, "Donner à vivre," in *Le Surréalisme en 1947* (Paris: Editions Pierre à Feu, 1947), p. 67.

3. Jean Scutenaire, "Paul Delvaux," in *London Bulletin*, no. 3 (June 1938), p. 8.

4. In view of Surrealism's faith in the revelatory power of chance, it is worth noting that *L'Europe après la Pluie* was well advanced before Ernst had the opportunity to see the landscapes of Arizona, of which the rock formations in his pictures are so

reminiscent. See Patrick Waldberg, *Max Ernst* (Paris: Jean-Jacques Pauvert, 1958): "He made for Saint-Martin once more. His son Jimmy, from New York, was engaged in obtaining for him an entry visa to the United States. From Carcassonne, Joë Bousquet sent him a little money. It was at this moment that he painted his great landscapes, *L'Europe après la Pluie, L'Ange du Marécage, Le Miroir volé*" (p. 337).

5. Nicolas Calas, "The Light of Words," in *Arson, an Ardent Review, Part One of a Surrealist Manifestation* (London, 1942), p. 13.

6. Marco Ristitch in *Le Surréalisme au service de la Révolution*, no. VI (May 1933), p. 39.

7 PROSPECTING THE IMAGINARY

1. "Une Démolition au Platane," *Médium*, nouv. série, no. 4 (January 1955), p. 58.

2. "Le Congrès s'amuse," in *Médium*, nouv. série, no. 1 (November 1953), p. 16.

3. Edouard Jaguer, untitled statement, dated September 1960, in *Surrealist Intrusion in the Enchanters' Domain* (New York: D'Arcy Galleries, 1960), p. 25.

4. "In the Light of Surrealism," in Alfred H. Barr Jr., *Fantastic Art, Dada, Surrealism* (New York: The Museum of Modern Art, 3rd edition, 1947), p. 46.

5. "L'Art des Fous," in his *La Clé des Champs* (Paris: Les Editions du Sagittaire, 1953), p. 227.

6. See Paul Eluard, "Le Miroir de Baudelaire," in *Minotaure*, no. 1–2 (June 1933), p. 64.

7. See *Minotaure*, no. 3–4 (May 1934), p. 19.

8. Arthur Sale, "On the Trolley Bus," reproduced in the catalogue *Surrealist Objects and Poems* (London: London Gallery, n.d.).

8 THE ENCHANTERS' DOMAIN

1. *La Littérature au Défi: Aragon surréaliste* (Geneva: à la Baconnière, 1957), p. 77.

2. See the preface to his *Anthologie de la Poésie française depuis le Surréalisme* (Paris: Editions de Beaune, 1952), p. 7.

3. From Carrouges' reply to Gilbert Ganne's enquiry, "Qu'as-tu fait de ta jeunesse?" in *Arts*, no. 560 (March 21–27, 1956), p. 8.

4. On June 16 1936, Breton participated in the series of lectures delivered on the occasion of the International Surrealist Exhibition, at the Conway Hall, London. His talk, "Limites non Frontières du Surréalisme," was published in English in Herbert Read's symposium, *Surrealism* (London: Faber, 1936), and in French in *La Nouvelle Revue française*, no. 281 (February 1937).

5. Edouard Jaguer, untitled statement in *Surrealist Intrusion in the Enchanters' Domain* (New York: D'Arcy Galleries, 1960), p. 25.

6. See "Le Château étoilé," in *Minotaure*, no. 8 (June 1936), p. 31.

7. Preface to his *Le Musée Noir* (1946). See *Le Musée Noir, Soleil des Loups* (Paris: Jean-Jacques Pauvert, 1957), p. 5.

8. *Médium*, nouv. série, no. 4 (January 1955), p. 45.

9. See José Pierre, "Kandinsky et Chirico," in *Le Surréalisme, même*, no. 2 (1957), p. 40.

10. *International Surrealist Bulletin*, no. 4 (September 1936), p. 12.

11. "La Liberté du langage," in the catalogue *Le Surréalisme en 1947* (Paris: Editions Pierre à Feu, 1947), p. 61.

12. "Physique de la poésie," in *Minotaure*, no. 6 (December 1934), p. 6.

13. "Lozanne," in *Man's Life is This Meat* (London: The Parton Press, 1936).

14. Si seulement il faisait du soleil cette nuit
Si dans le fond de l'Opéra deux seins miroitants et clairs
Composaient pour le mot amour la plus merveilleuse
    lettrine vivante

(If only there were sunshine tonight
If behind the Opera two shining bright breasts
Composed for the word love the most marvellous
    living capital letter)

15. Gascoyne, "And the Seventh Dream is the Dream of Isis," in *Man's Life is This Meat*.

16. Victor Bounoure, "Surrealism and the Savage Heart," in *Surrealist Intrusion in the Enchanters' Domain* (New York: D'Arcy Galleries, 1960), p. 28.

17. René Crevel, review of Max Ernst, *Histoire naturelle* (1926), in *La Nouvelle Revue française,* October 1927, p. 554.

18. A. C. Sewter, "Projection," reproduced in the catalogue *Surrealist Objects and Poems* (London: London Gallery, n.d.).

19. Quoted in *Surrealist Intrusion in the Enchanters' Domain,* p. 84.

20. "The New Image," in *Dyn,* no. 1 (1942), p. 13.

21. Cited in Peggy Guggenheim (ed.), *Art of This Century* (New York: Art of This Century, 1942), p. 118.

22. "The World of René Magritte," in *The Saturday Book,* no. 19 (1959), p. 274.

23. See *Fantasmagie,* no. 3–4 (1959), p. 59.

24. See "Le Fil d'Ariane," in *Documents 34,* nouv. série no. 1 ("Intervention surréaliste," June 1934), p. 15.

9 THE GRAND BATTUE OF DESIRE

1. See Charles Estienne and José Pierre, "Situation de la peinture en 1954," in *Médium,* nouv. série, no. 4 (January 1955), p. 45.

2. Georges Goldfayn, in *Médium,* première série, no. 7 (May 1953).

3. See the tract "Hands off Love," reprinted in *transition* in 1927.

4. In *La Révolution surréaliste,* no. 11 (March 1928).

5. In *Médium,* nouv. série, no. 3 (May 1954, number dedicated to Svanberg), p. 2.

6. Man Ray has painted an *Imaginary Portrait of D. A. F. Sade,* Jean Benoit a *Hommage au Marquis de Sade.* Jindrich Heisler has designed a frontispiece for *La Philosophie dans le Boudoir.* Heine and Lely have both written poems dedicated to Sade.

7. This meeting
With everything that from a distance is fatal in it
This rushing together of two systems considered

separately as subjective
Sets off a series of very real phenomena
That take part in the formation of a distinct world
Of a kind to bring shame on what we would perceive
Without it.

8. What then is this distant country
That seems to draw all its light from your life
Very real it trembles on the edge of your eyelashes.

9. "Dans les eaux du rêve et le feu de l'action," in *Cahiers GLM*,
Septième Cahier (March 1938), p. 94.

10. And always one single couple united in a single garment
By the same desire
Lying at the feet of their reflection
A limitless couple.

11. *Les Cahiers du Sud*, no. 337 ("Pour Saluer Crevel," 1956),
p. 348.

12. My flaming plane castle soaked in Rhenish wine
ghetto of black irises ear of cristal
rock running down the cliff to crush the policeman.
The complete text of this poem, with accompanying transla-
tion, appears in J. H. Matthews, *Péret's Score: Vingt Poèmes
de Benjamin Péret* (Paris: Lettres Modernes, 1964).

13. Georges Henein, "Histoire vague," in *VVV*, no. 4 (1944),
p. 62.

14. The point of your eyes
On the points of your breasts
Your eyes in my breast
And your breasts in my head
At the hour when nothing lies in wait for us in the mirror
I leave by the long path where nothing can stop me any more.

15. Flights of parrots pass through my head when I see you in
profile
and the sky of grease is streaked with blue lightning
that traces your name in all directions.
Péret, "Clin d'œil," in *Je Sublime* (1936).

16. The tender paths traced by your bright blood
Links creatures together
It is a moss covering the desert
Without night ever being able to leave upon it
impression or rut.
"L'Entente," in *Facile* (1935).

10 CONCLUSION

1. See *Surrealist Intrusion in the Enchanters' Domain* (New York: D'Arcy Galleries, 1960), p. 83.

2. "Painting is a Wager," in *Horizon*, VII, no. 38 (March 1943), p. 183.

3. *Médium, nouv. série*, no. 4 (Number dedicated to Lam, January 1955), p. 1.

4. "Amour, révolte et poésie," in the catalogue *Le Surréalisme en 1947* (Paris: Editions Pierre à Feu, 1947), p. 100.

5. Julien Gracq, *André Breton: Quelques Aspects de l'Ecrivain* (Paris: José Corti, 1948), p. 122.

6. "Donner à vivre," in *Le Surréalisme en 1947*, p. 66.

7. "L'Homme emblématique," in *VVV*, no. 1 (June 1942), p. 10:
   At the centre of the world is man
   He is the point the circle and the ray
   From top to bottom his whole frame
   By a very pure sword is traversed.

8. "Qu'as-tu fait de ta jeunesse?" in *Arts*, no. 560 (March 21–27, 1956), p. 8.

9. "Farewell to Surrealism," in *Dyn*, no. 1 (1942), p. 26.

10. See his "Déposition," in *Les Cahiers du Mois*, no. 21–22 (1926).

11. See *Surrealist Intrusion in the Enchanters' Domain*, p. 124.

12. *Ibid.*, p. 44.

13. The text of Breton's talk at Yale University, "Situation du Surréalisme entre les deux guerres," was printed in *Yale French Studies*, I, no. 2 (Fall–Winter 1948). It had already been printed in Paris by the review *Fontaine* in 1945.

14. See Breton's interview in *Le Monde*, January 13, 1962.

15. Corneille, in *Médium*, nouv. série, no. 4 (January 1955), p. 50.

16. Published in the review *Commerce* in 1924, Aragon's article was published separately ("hors 'Commerce'") in the same year.

SUGGESTED READING

BOOKS

BALAKIAN, Anna. *Literary Origins of Surrealism: A New Mysticism in French Poetry.* New York: King's Crown Press, 1947.

BRETON, André. *What is Surrealism?* London: Faber, 1936.

CARMODY, Francis J., and McINTYRE, Carlysle, *Surrealist Poetry in France.* Berkeley: California Book Co., 1955.

GASCOYNE, David. *A Short Survey of Surrealism.* London: Cobden Sanderson, 1935.

JEAN, Marcel. *The History of Surrealist Painting.* New York: Grove Press, 1960.

LEMAITRE, Georges E. *From Cubism to Surrealism in French Literature.* Cambridge, Mass.: Harvard University Press, 1941.

LEVY, Julien (ed.). *Surrealism.* New York: The Black Sun Press, 1936.

LESAGE, Laurent. *Jean Giraudoux, Surrealism and the German Romantic Ideal.* Urbana: University of Illinois Press, 1952.

NEAGOE, Peter. *What is Surrealism?* Paris: New Review Publications, 1932.

READ, Herbert (ed.). *Surrealism*. New York: Harcourt Brace, 1936.

WALDBERG, Patrick. *Surrealism*. Geneva: Skira, 1962 (distributed by the World Publishing Company, Cleveland, Ohio).

ENGLISH-LANGUAGE SURREALIST REVIEWS

London Bulletin, London, 1938–40 (twenty issues).

Arson, London, 1942 (one issue).

VVV, New York, 1942–44 (four issues).

Free Unions, London, 1946 (one issue).

Bulletin International du Surréalisme. Fourth and last bulletin appeared in London, in bilingual text, in September 1936.

OTHER COLLECTIVE PUBLICATIONS IN ENGLISH

Surrealist Objects and Poems. London: London Gallery Editions [1937].

BRETON, André, and DUCHAMP, Marcel. *First Papers of Surrealism*. New York: Co-ordinating Council of French Relief Societies, 1942.

MESENS, E. L. T. (ed.). *Message from Nowhere*. London: London Gallery Editions, 1944.

SURREALIST ISSUES OF ENGLISH-LANGUAGE REVIEWS

Contemporary Poetry and Prose, London, no. 2 (June 1936).

New Directions in Prose and Poetry, Norfolk, Conn. (1940).

New Road, Billericay, Essex (1943).

This Quarter, Paris (September 1932).

View, New York, no. 7–8 (October–November 1941).

Yale French Studies, no. 31 (May 1964).

INDEX